Michael Collins

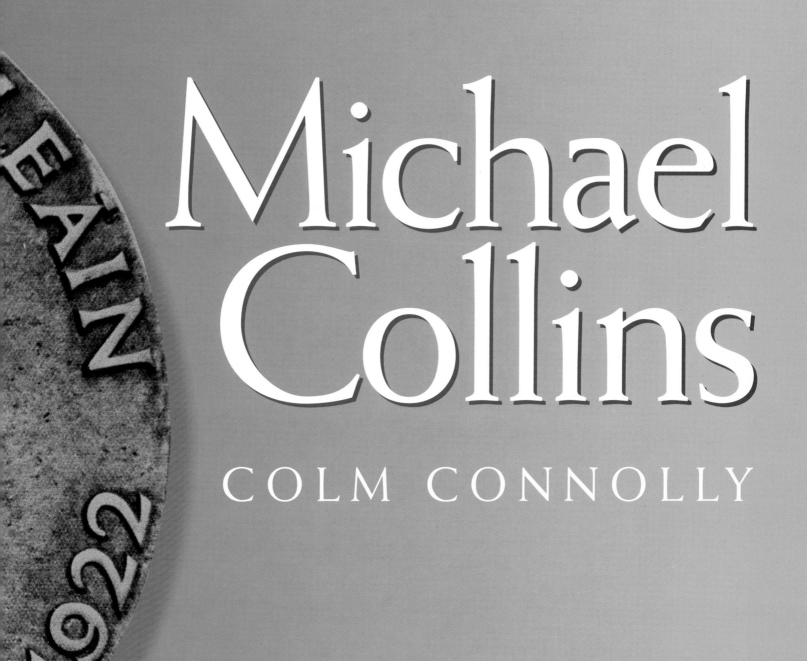

Michael Collins

COLM CONNOLLY

WEIDENFELD & NICOLSON

LONDON

CONTENTS

The

Beginnings

When Collins was just six years old,

his father died after a heart attack.

On his deathbed, he pointed to

Michael junior and said to the

assembled family: 'Mind that child.

He'll be a great man yet and will do

things for Ireland'.

Michael Collins aged about nine with his (far right) mother, grandmother, sister and brother outside the family home.

Years later, speaking about efforts to achieve his political goal, Collins would recall how these men infused him with pride

Michael Collins was born into a humble but comfortable family home at Woodfield near Clonakilty in West Cork, a beautiful but remote area of Ireland's southernmost county.

The simple, small, thatched house stood on farmland near Sam's Cross, a meeting of roads named after Sam Wallace, a highwayman of yesteryear, whose Robin Hood-like activities earned the gratitude of the locals and the deep hatred of the landed gentry.

Mary Anne (Marianne) O'Brien was only 23 when she married her family's 60-year-old neighbour, Michael John Collins. For both of them, it would be beneficial: he would have a young and healthy woman to look after the household, which also included his three brothers, and she would have a husband who held about 35 hectares (90 acres) of land on which he raised cows, pigs and sheep. In all, Mary Anne and John would have eight children – five girls and three boys. The last of them, Michael Patrick, arrived in the early hours of 16 October, 1890.

This boy inherited his father's love of good books and learning which the elderly farmer had, in turn, acquired from a cousin, a 'hedge school' teacher. Such men had travelled the country and defied the penal laws before Catholic emancipation by teaching children reading, writing and mathematics on the roadside, often under the shelter of hedges.

In his own education, the young Michael would suffer no such hardships. He attended Lisavaird National School, 3 kilometres (2 miles) from the homestead, where his teacher, Denis Lyons, nurtured the flame of nationalism already lit in the boy by members of his family. Lyons was a member of a secret organization, the Irish Republican Brotherhood, sworn to obtain independence for Ireland, using armed force if necessary.

Another influence was James Santry, a local blacksmith, whose grandfather had taken part in the 1798 Rebellion and whose father had forged pikes for the risings of 1848 and 1867. Rural forges were often meeting points for people from wide spreads of countryside, and Michael would spend many hours listening to Santry and his customers exchanging stories of rebellion, hangings, famine and harsh evictions.

Years later, speaking about efforts to achieve his political goal, Collins would recall how these men infused him with pride in the Irish as a race: 'Denis Lyons and James Santry remain to me my first stalwarts'.

When Collins was just six years old, his father died after a heart attack. On his deathbed, he pointed to Michael junior and said to the assembled family: 'Mind that child. He'll be a great man yet and will do things for Ireland'.

Three years after her husband's death, Collins' mother employed local stonemasons and carpenters to build a new house for the family, alongside the old.

For the boy, there were other preoccupations. He loved the outdoor life – wildly galloping the family pony over the farmland, fishing in rivers and streams, and splashing in the Atlantic surf on nearby Black Strand, although, strangely, he never learned to swim. His abiding passion was a rough-and-tumble form of wrestling known as 'grabbing a bit of ear'. The contest ended only when one of the combatants was unable to continue. Michael, sturdy and fiercely competitive, usually won. Defeat infuriated him.

After National School, Collins went to Clonakilty for 18 months to study for the Post Office entrance examination, staying with his sister, Margaret, whose husband owned a local newspaper.

In 1906, at the age of 15, he passed the Boy Clerkship test and was sent to London to take up a position at the Post Office Savings Bank in West Kensington. His sister Johanna ('Hannie') was already in London working for the Post Office, and he stayed with her for the next nine years, living over a shop at 5 Netherwood Road, West Kensington. As with many exiles from rural Ireland, he was lonely in the unfamiliar city and readily became involved in the home-from-home activities of his fellow immigrants, such as ceilidhes and membership of the Gaelic League, which promoted the use of the Irish language.

His niece, Una Mulhearn, told the author that Hannie thought he was wild and unruly when he first arrived in London, and she had her hands full in controlling his boisterous nature. Thankfully for Hannie, he channelled his energy into field sports, joining the Gaelic Athletic Association to play football and hurling. What he lacked in skill was more than compensated for in fiery temperament. He was more proficient in athletic pursuits: he won a GAA gold medal for the 440-yards hurdle race. He became secretary of his local club, the Geraldines, and later took over the financial reins of the entire London branch of the GAA.

Less than a year after leaving home, his mother died of cancer. Neither he nor Hannie had sufficient funds to make the journey to Cork for the funeral. How the death of his second parent and his inability to physically join his family in mourning affected the young man, one can only imagine.

Collins still yearned for Irish independence and had no time for the Irish Parliamentary Party in the House of Commons, whose members he considered to be 'slaves of England'. He did, however, admire greatly the writings of Arthur Griffith in the newspaper *United Irishman*. Griffith had founded his own political party, Sinn Féin (We Ourselves), in 1905.

Three years after leaving Cork, Collins became a member of the Irish Republican Brotherhood, sworn in by his fellow Post Office worker, Sam Maguire, in November, 1909. Collins would later become IRB treasurer for London and the South of England. The seeds of revolutionary nationalism, sown by a West Cork blacksmith and a schoolteacher, had borne fruit.

In 1910, Collins moved from the Post Office to a stockbroking firm, Horne & Co, in Moorgate Street, and then, in 1914, to the Board of Trade as a clerk. His stay there was brief, and he took up employment in the London branch of the Guaranty Trust Company of New York in the following year.

Physically, Michael Collins was now a fine young man, robust and handsome and just a little short of 1.8 metres (6 feet) tall. It was around this time that he gained the nickname 'The Big Fellow'. 'It wasn't just because he was big in stature', his nephew, Lieutenant-

Michael Collins photographed after his return to Ireland from Frongoch Camp.

General Sean Collins-Powell, told the author. 'Indeed, there were many of his companions who were taller and stronger. Some people called him The Big Fellow because he would willingly undertake any job, no matter how difficult. Others used the nickname sarcastically because, according to them, he was a bit of a show-off.'

Collins was seldom bereft of female attention and he had several girlfriends during his years in the English capital. A strong jaw, dark brown hair hanging in a kiss curl over grey-blue eyes that could narrow threateningly or just as quickly twinkle with a boyish smile, together with his physique, were to capture hearts. But time for flirtation was limited by his many other activities.

Three months before the outbreak of World War I, he had enrolled as an Irish Volunteer, drilling with No. 1 Company in a hall in King's Cross. Early in 1916, the second year of the Great War, he told his employers he was going to join his unit. They, naturally, understood him to mean a unit of the British army but he knew he would soon be fighting against that army in Ireland. His IRB contacts had told him a rising was being planned.

In Dublin, he found work with an accountancy firm, Craig, Gardner & Company, and spent much of his leisure time helping the secret activities of the IRB and training with the Irish Volunteers.

POBLACHT NA H EIREANN.

THE PROVISIONAL GOVERNMENT
OF THE
IRISH REPUBLIC
TO THE PEOPLE OF IRELAND.

IRISHMEN AND IRISHWOMEN: In the name of God and of the dead generations from which she receives her old tradition of nationhood, Ireland, through us, summons her children to her flag and strikes for her freedom.

Having organised and trained her manhood through her secret revolutionary organisation, the Irish Republican Brotherhood, and through her open military organisations, the Irish Volunteers and the Irish Citizen Army, having patiently perfected her discipline, having resolutely waited for the right moment to reveal itself, she now seizes that moment, and, supported by her exiled children in America and by gallant allies in Europe, but relying in the first on her own strength, she strikes in full confidence of victory.

We declare the right of the people of Ireland to the ownership of Ireland, and to the unfettered control of Irish destinies, to be sovereign and indefeasible. The long usurpation of that right by a foreign people and government has not extinguished the right, nor can it ever be extinguished except by the destruction of the Irish people. In every generation the Irish people have asserted their right to national freedom and sovereignty: six times during the past three hundred years they have asserted it in arms. Standing on that fundamental right and again asserting it in arms in the face of the world, we hereby proclaim the Irish Republic as a Sovereign Independent State, and we pledge our lives and the lives of our comrades-in-arms to the cause of its freedom, of its welfare, and of its exaltation among the nations.

The Irish Republic is entitled to, and hereby claims, the allegiance of every Irishman and Irishwoman. The Republic guarantees religious and civil liberty, equal rights and equal opportunities to all its citizens, and declares its resolve to pursue the happiness and prosperity of the whole nation and of all its parts, cherishing all the children of the nation equally, and oblivious of the differences carefully fostered by an alien government, which have divided a minority from the majority in the past.

Until our arms have brought the opportune moment for the establishment of a permanent National Government, representative of the whole people of Ireland and elected by the suffrages of all her men and women, the Provisional Government, hereby constituted, will administer the civil and military affairs of the Republic in trust for the people.

We place the cause of the Irish Republic under the protection of the Most High God, Whose blessing we invoke upon our arms, and we pray that no one who serves that cause will dishonour it by cowardice, inhumanity, or rapine. In this supreme hour the Irish nation must, by its valour and discipline and by the readiness of its children to sacrifice themselves for the common good, prove itself worthy of the august destiny to which it is called.

Signed on Behalf of the Provisional Government,

THOMAS J. CLARKE.

SEAN Mac DIARMADA. THOMAS MacDONAGH.
P. H. PEARSE. EAMONN CEANNT.
JAMES CONNOLLY. JOSEPH PLUNKETT.

The Rising

'We declare the right of the people of

Ireland to the ownership of Ireland, and

the unfettered control of Irish destinies,

to be sovereign and indefeasible . . . .'

The supreme council of the Irish Republican Brotherhood had decided in September, 1914 – the early weeks of World War I – that an insurrection would take place in Ireland during this conflict between Great Britain and Germany.

A split in the Irish Volunteers had resulted in 170,000 staying loyal to John Redmond's Irish Parliamentary Party, which had been promised home rule for Ireland if Irishmen served Britain in the trenches. The remaining 10,000, under the command of Eoin MacNeil, a university professor and president of the Gaelic League, were regarded by the Irish Republican Brotherhood as the nucleus for a rising. A fifth of this number was based in Dublin, where it would be augmented by the Citizen Army, a militia led by James Connolly, a socialist and trade union activist. The Army had been formed originally to protect workers from a repeat of the brutality meted out by the police during a general strike the previous year. Connolly would serve as second-in-command to Padraic Pearse, poet, schoolteacher and separatist. And Staff Captain Michael Collins would act as aide-de-camp to Joseph Plunkett, another of the leaders.

Easter Monday, 24 April, 1916, was the day chosen for the rebellion. Other areas throughout the

FAR RIGHT Group of Irish Volunteers photographed at a training camp in North County Dublin in 1912.

Members of the Fianna Eireann (Boy Scout Branch of Irish Volunteers) waiting to unload rifles and ammunition at Howth, Co. Dublin in 1914. The munitions were brought from Germany on board the yacht 'Asgard', owned by Erskine Childers who would be executed 7 years later in the Civil War.

Group of Irish Volunteers photographed in Dublin's St Stephen's Green on the day before the Rising.

RIGHT Willie and Padraic Pearse photographed at St. Enda's school, Dublin where they educated boys through the medium of the Irish language. Both were executed for their part in the 1916 Rising.

country were intended to rise also but, as a result of general confusion and countermanded orders, the insurrection was confined largely to Dublin. Militarily, it could not succeed.

The combined rebel force totalled fewer than 2,000 men and women. The latter, members of the Cumann na mBan (women's branch) of the Irish Volunteers, numbered about a hundred. These women served as nurses, couriers and secretaries. Initially ranged against this force were 2,500 British troops in the Dublin area, reinforced within 48 hours by 2,000 soldiers who were landed from England at Kingstown (now Dun Laoghaire) harbour. In addition, there were 9,500 armed members of the Royal Irish Constabulary.

The holiday weekend had been bathed in warm, spring sunshine and thousands of city-dwellers had travelled daily to the beaches and mountains. Many British soldiers had been given leave, and most of their officers had gone to The Curragh in County Kildare to enjoy the race meeting there – one of the highlights of the Irish social calendar.

At twelve noon, Pearse and Connolly marched their men to the General Post Office, a Palladian building dominating the city's main thoroughfare, Sackville Street (now O'Connell Street). This would be the general headquarters of the rebels. Other units took control of buildings and areas commanding the entrance to the city. Boland's Mill, a bakery on the south side was commandeered by Eamon de Valera, a mathematics teacher. He would figure greatly in Michael Collins' life in the future.

At twelve noon, Pearse and Connolly marched their men to the General Post Office

'We declare the right of the people of Ireland to the ownership of Ireland . . . to be . . . indefeasible'

Padraic Pearse stood outside the GPO and read the proclamation of the Provisional Government of the Irish Republic, drawn up by him and his six fellow signatories: 'We declare the right of the people of Ireland to the ownership of Ireland, and the unfettered control of Irish destinies, to be sovereign and indefeasible . . . .'

The few Dubliners who stopped to listen to Pearse were bemused by his words and, more especially, by the actions of volunteers inside the building who were smashing windows and erecting barricades of furniture and mailbags. Two flags, one with the words 'Irish Republic' on a green background and the other a tricolour, white and orange, were raised on the roof.

Later that afternoon, a group of British army lancers arrived at the top of the street and advanced, in battle formation, on the GPO. A volley of rifle fire from the building killed four of the mounted soldiers. The remainder galloped away in disorder.

Brigadier-General W.H.M. Lowe was in command of British forces in Dublin. He asked for, and was given in the coming days, an additional 4,000 soldiers from different parts of Ireland. On Tuesday, the gunboat 'Helga' moved up the River Liffey and began shelling Liberty Hall, the headquarters of Connolly's Citizen Army and his trade union. The following day, the boat extended its shelling to Sackville Street and

FAR LEFT
Ruins of the General Post Office after the 1916 Rising. James Connolly was wounded in the street running along the left side of the building.

British Troops inspect the burnt out shell of the GPO.

From Commander of Dublin Forces
To P. H. Pearce
                          29. April/16
                                1.40 P.M.
A woman has come in and tells me
you wish to negotiate with me.
I am prepared to receive you in
BRITAIN ST. at the North End of
MOORE ST provided that you
surrender unconditionally —
You will proceed up MOORE ST
accompanied only by the woman who
brings you this note under a white
flag —

The O'Rahilly was shot down as he led a desperate charge from the burning GPO.

ABOVE RIGHT The note sent to Commandant Padraic Pearse by General Lowe after Pearse's offer to surrender.

the GPO, joined by army artillery batteries placed at vantage points around the city.

Brigadier-General Lowe concentrated the big guns on the rebel headquarters before putting more weight against the outposts. The strategy worked. By Thursday, most of the buildings in Sackville Street and the surrounding area were in flames. James Connolly's ankle had been shattered by a bullet when he left the GPO to reconnoitre British positions. Hit also in the elbow before being dragged back into the building, he was now

It was a desperate effort by desperate men

confined to a stretcher. He was just one of many casualties, inside and outside the GPO building.

By Thursday afternoon, it was obvious that the rebel headquarters could not be held. The building was in flames and the roof had fallen in. Padraic Pearse ordered the Cumann na mBan, with the exception of three women, to leave.

On Friday evening, one of the leaders, Michael O'Rahilly ('The O'Rahilly'), led 12 volunteers in a charge on the barricade at the end of Moore Street, which ran parallel to O'Connell Street. If they could overrun this position they could gain access for the

GPO garrison to a factory building beyond the flames. It was a desperate effort by desperate men.

As they charged the barricade 165 metres (180 yards) away, two volunteers immediately behind O'Rahilly, Shortiss and Cremmins, were hit by gunfire. Shortiss died instantly but Cremmins, hit in the leg, managed to drag himself into a building. The others took shelter in empty houses and shops.

When the charging volunteers were only about 30 metres (33 yards) from the barricade, O'Rahilly was hit twice but managed to get across the road into a lane and out of the line of fire. As he lay dying, he

Commandant Eamon de Valera (marked 'x') leads the Boland's Mill contingent into captivity, escorted by British soldiers.

ABOVE
Joseph, George and John Plunkett, sons of Count Plunkett, under arrest at Richmond Barracks in Dublin after the Rising. Joseph, one of the signatories of the Proclamation of Independence, was executed by firing squad in Kilmainham gaol.

James Connolly, the Scottish-born leader of the Irish Citizen Army, who was strapped into a wicker-work armchair to be shot by firing squad.

scribbled a final pencilled note to his wife: 'Darling Nancy, I was shot leading a rush . . . I got more than one bullet I think . . . It was a good fight anyhow . . . Goodbye darling.'

Later that night, the remainder of the GPO garrison dashed in groups from the side of the building, carrying Connolly and the other injured – including a captured British soldier – through machine gun and rifle fire, to find shelter in houses in neighbouring streets. One man was killed and 17 wounded during this evacuation.

The rebels began burrowing through the walls of

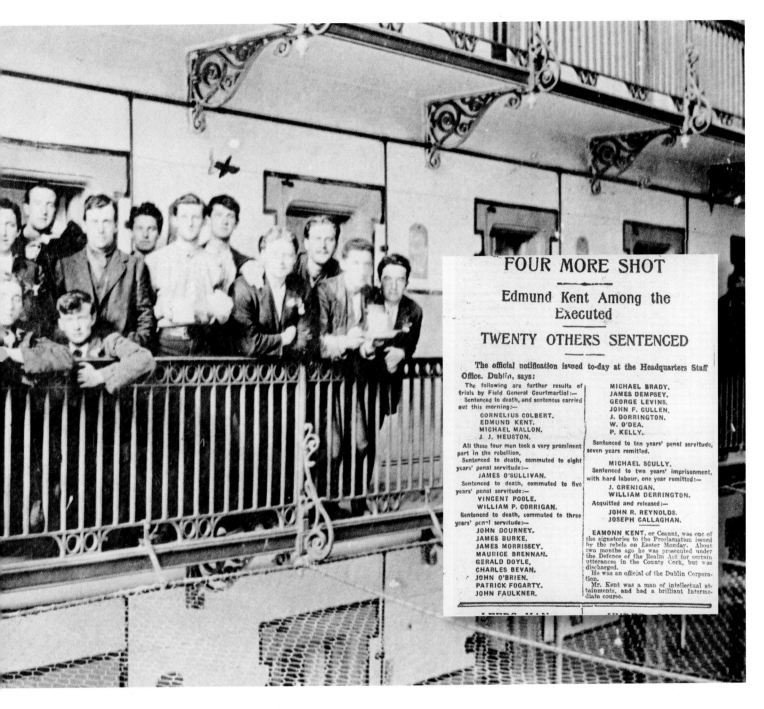

FOUR MORE SHOT

Edmund Kent Among the Executed

TWENTY OTHERS SENTENCED

The official notification issued to-day at the Headquarters Staff Office, Dublin, says:

The following are further results of trials by Field General Courtmartial:— Sentenced to death, and sentences carried out this morning:—

CORNELIUS COLBERT.
EDMUND KENT.
MICHAEL MALLON.
J. J. HEUSTON.

All these four men took a very prominent part in the rebellion.

Sentenced to death, commuted to eight years' penal servitude:—

JAMES O'SULLIVAN.

Sentenced to death, commuted to five years' penal servitude:—

VINCENT POOLE.
WILLIAM P. CORRIGAN.

Sentenced to death, commuted to three years' penal servitude:—

JOHN DOURNEY.
JAMES BURKE.
JAMES MORRISSEY.
MAURICE BRENNAN.
GERALD DOYLE.
CHARLES BEVAN.
JOHN O'BRIEN.
PATRICK FOGARTY.
JOHN FAULKNER.

MICHAEL BRADY.
JAMES DEMPSEY.
GEORGE LEVINS.
JOHN F. CULLEN.
J. DORRINGTON.
W. O'DEA.
P. KELLY.

Sentenced to ten years' penal servitude, seven years remitted.

MICHAEL SCULLY.

Sentenced to two years' imprisonment, with hard labour, one year remitted:—

J. CRENIGAN.
WILLIAM DERRINGTON.

Acquitted and released:—

JOHN R. REYNOLDS.
JOSEPH CALLAGHAN.

EAMONN KENT, or Ceannt, was one of the signatories to the Proclamation issued by the rebels on Easter Monday. About two months ago he was prosecuted under the Defence of the Realm Act for certain utterances in the County Cork, but was discharged.

He was an official of the Dublin Corporation.

Mr. Kent was a man of intellectual attainments, and had a brilliant Intermediate course.

the houses, moving from building to building in a last bid to bypass the cordon of British troops, but this only added to the agony of the wounded and the fatigue of the tunnellers. They could smell the smoke of the burning buildings around them and hear the relentless firing of machine guns and rifles from the encircling barricades. Occasionally, they could feel the concussive thud of hand grenades.

A council of war was held by the rebel leaders on the morning of Saturday, 29 April. They would try to negotiate surrender terms.

Volunteer nurse Elizabeth ('Liz') O'Farrell, one of the three remaining Cumann na mBan members, was asked to take a verbal message to the British. A makeshift white flag was hung from a window of the house and firing by the British gradually stopped. Carrying another white flag and wearing her nurse's uniform, Liz stepped slowly from the building and walked up to the barricade at the top of Moore Street. There a British officer accused her of being a spy and ordered a second officer to cut the red crosses from her arm and apron. She was then held by the British troops in a tobacconist's shop for an hour and a half until Brigadier-General Lowe arrived. He said he

Michael Collins, photographed on balcony in Stafford Gaol after the 1916 Rising.

INSET
As the news of the executions and sentencing was reported, in this case *The Evening Herald*, British authorities seemed indifferent to the growing feeling of revulsion among the public.

would not treat at all until Pearse and the rebels surrendered unconditionally.

At half-past three that afternoon, Padraic Pearse, accompanied by Liz O'Farrell, met Brigadier-General Lowe at the corner of Moore Street and Parnell Street. The general's son, John, who was also an officer serving in the British army, accompanied his father to witness the surrender. (John Lowe later changed his surname to Loder and became a successful film producer in Hollywood.)

Pearse reluctantly handed up his sword to the brigadier-general. Liz O'Farrell then carried Pearse's message of surrender to rebel commanders in outposts around the city. 'In order to prevent the further slaughter of Dublin citizens, and in the hope of saving the lives of our followers now surrounded and hopelessly outnumbered, members of the Provisional Government present at headquarters have agreed to an unconditional surrender, and the commandants of the various districts in the city and county will order their commands to lay down arms. (Signed) P. H. Pearse, 29 April, 1916, 3.45 pm.'

As the rebels were marched away, they were jeered by onlookers. Many Dubliners had relatives serving with the British army overseas and they saw the rising as a stab in the back.

The damage to the city centre and surrounding areas was enormous. Entire blocks had been shelled and burned out. Over the coming months, the skeletons of these once-gracious buildings were pulled down. Fire and damage claims totalling £3 million were lodged at City Hall.

Exact casualty figures have never been established for the week of fighting, but estimates indicated that about 1,350 people were killed or wounded. The official British army casualty list gave a total of 516 officers and men killed, wounded or missing.

The civilian population suffered 364 deaths. Some 850 men, women and children were wounded.

But the killing was not over yet. Sixteen of the

Internees behind the wire. Michael Collins was one of 1,832 men held after the rising.

'that valiant effort and the martyrdoms that followed it finally awoke the sleeping spirit of Ireland'.

leaders of the rebellion were court-martialled and executed. Fifteen were shot, including James Connolly, who, unable to stand, was lifted from a stretcher and strapped into a chair to face the firing squad.

Sir Roger Casement was hanged in London at the same time. He was an Irish patriot, knighted by the British for his services to the diplomatic service. Having joined the Irish Volunteers, he sought aid in the USA and Germany for the Irish uprising. He was arrested by the British and tried for high treason.

Michael Collins said of the 1916 Rising: 'It appeared at the time of the surrender to have failed, but that valiant effort and the martyrdoms that followed it finally awoke the sleeping spirit of Ireland'.

The killing of the leaders by the British was, perhaps, understandable in the climate of the Great War. However, those executions in Kilmainham gaol, Dublin, over a period of ten days, shifted public opinion in Ireland from anger to sympathy for the rebels and a burning resentment towards representatives of the Crown.

As a result, largely, of that dangerous sway, 97 people had their death sentences commuted. Eamon de Valera escaped the firing squad because of his American citizenship. Five women and 1,832 men were interned in England. Among them was 26-year-old Michael Collins who, as Irish Prisoner No 48F, was sent with 237 others to Stafford Gaol on 1 May, 1916.

Irish Volunteers leaving Frongoch Camp to return to Ireland.

Spies and

Auxiliaries being inspected by General Tudor, head of the reconstituted police force, with the Lord
Lieutenant-General of Ireland, Field Marshall Lord French.

Apostles

The 'G' men working for Collins were invaluable. They advised him on the 'mentality' of the intelligence establishment, how it operated and, especially, what it planned to prevent a recurrence of armed rebellion. Dublin Castle, like many in Sinn Féin and the Irish Volunteers, assumed there would be a standing battle similar to 1916. But Collins was planning something far more widespread and devastating.

'We have not lost. To refuse to fight would have been to lose. To fight is to win.'

Michael Collins was transferred to an internment camp at Frongoch, North Wales, in June, 1916, and here he formed friendships with men who shared not only his ideal of Irish freedom but also his ideas about how this could be achieved.

In his address to the court martial, Padraic Pearse had said: 'We seem to have lost. We have not lost. To refuse to fight would have been to lose. To fight is to win'. Collins agreed only with the sentiment.

The Rising, like others in previous centuries, had been a bloody and noble sacrifice that stirred the Irish conscience and allowed patriotic fervour to bubble over. And, as before, those emotions would soon settle again into a resigned, helpless stupor. Collins was still convinced that physical force was the only way to get independence, but he believed that a new form of fighting would have to be employed. Conventional, pitched battles against numerically superior forces were foolhardy and costly. He would develop and modify the hit-and-run tactics of the Boers in South Africa, that is, guerrilla warfare.

Outwardly, Collins was a gregarious, if sometimes short-tempered, young man. He was well built and fond of physical sports, although also given to the study of literature. A loudmouth at times, and a bit of a bully, if allowed, he was to most of those interned with him, however, just one of the lads. These characteristics were very real, but he cultivated a simplistic façade and used it, tactically, on friend and foe in the years ahead. He was already choosing from among this disparate body not only those who would share his military and political policies, but those who could be entrusted with either the public or the clandestine work he planned. This 'horses-for-courses' selectivity would be one of his great strengths.

The first batch of internees, including Michael Collins, was released from Frongoch at Christmas, 1916. He travelled from Dublin to Woodfield saddened by the death of his grandmother the previous day. His visit was a disappointment. His old friends in the area, who had not shared his experiences in Dublin and, of course, imprisonment, were unable to comprehend fully his emotional state and his desire to re-enter the fray so soon after the Rising. After three weeks, he was glad to return to Dublin.

He had been given the job of secretary-accountant of the National Aid Association, which was set up to help the dependants of those who had died fighting in the Rising, or to give financial support to the Volunteers themselves and find them jobs.

While other Volunteers were celebrating their freedom after internment in Britain, Collins was secretly selecting his lieutenants for the struggle ahead. Some would operate in the public arena but others in his 'secret war'.

**Military checkpoints
became familiar
features of life in
Dublin and
throughout the
country. Generally,
the military enjoyed
a good relationship
with the civilian
population.**

It was an ideal situation for Collins. He had a position of influence nationally and a legitimate office from which he could reorganize the Irish Volunteers. He was now also a member of the supreme council of the Irish Republican Brotherhood and, as such, would become the central conduit for espionage intelligence from IRB sources throughout the country.

As well as his National Aid work, he began helping the revitalization of Arthur Griffith's party, Sinn Féin. In February, 1917, he and Griffith travelled to North Roscommon to campaign for Count Plunkett, an elderly scholar, in a by-election contest with an Irish Parliamentary Party candidate. Plunkett was the father of Collins' immediate superior in the GPO in 1916, Joseph Plunkett, who had been executed after the Rising. As well as Sinn Féin, Count Plunkett was supported by members of the Irish Volunteers and various Irish Parliamentary Party dissidents who had become dissaffected with John Redmond's attempts to achieve home rule by political agitation. Plunkett won the election by a huge majority.

Many of those who supported Plunkett, including Michael Collins, were opposed to Griffith's 'dual monarchy' philosophy which proposed an independent Ireland sharing a common king with Great Britain. However, all were united in their common detestation of Redmond's Home Rulers and, more importantly for Griffith and Collins, the opposition to the Irish Parliamentary Party was perceived by the general public to be Sinn Féin. Dozens of new branches were formed, and by the end of 1917 there were about 150,000 members.

Michael Collins and Harry Boland (right), rivals in love as well as in politics.

In May, 1917, Collins was again canvassing, this time in Longford for Joseph McGuinness, a 1916 prisoner still being held in Lewes gaol in England. Collins masterminded a poster campaign which showed McGuinness in prison uniform with the accompanying caption: 'Put him in to get him out'. He was put in, but only by a margin of 37 votes.

It was at this time that Collins met the great love of his life, Kitty Kiernan. During the Longford by-election campaign he stayed at the Greville Arms Hotel in Granard, County Longford. Katherine ('Kitty') Brigid Kiernan, was only 16 when her parents died and she, her three sisters and their brother took over the running of the family hotel, as well as the family's other businesses. These included a sizeable amount of the town's commerce – a bar, grocery shop,

hardware and timber store, a bakery and an undertaking establishment.

Kitty, although only the second-eldest, was the mainstay of the orphaned family. Attractive and vivacious, she enjoyed a busy life, entertaining in the hotel or visiting Dublin for the main events on the social calendar of the capital. When Collins first arrived in Granard, his close friend and colleague, Harry Boland, was already involved with Kitty, and it would be some time before she would switch her affections. Collins was initially attracted to Kitty's sister, Helen, but she chose to marry another.

Eamon de Valera, the only surviving commandant of the 1916 Rising, was part of the third group of internees released, in June, 1917. Dubliners gave them a rapturous reception and carried them on

The three men argued that, as they had been sentenced by a military court for political activity, they should have political status rather than be classified as common criminals. Ashe and about 40 similar prisoners went on hunger strike. As this was considered a breach of prison discipline, their boots, beds and bedding were taken from them. After six days, they were forcibly fed by prison staff, but the procedure on Ashe was botched and he had to be rushed, unconscious, to hospital. He died four days later.

Michael Collins organized the funeral of Thomas Ashe. The body was dressed in the uniform of the Irish Volunteers and laid out in City Hall with armed Volunteers standing guard. Tens of thousands of people filed past the coffin. On the day of Ashe's funeral, 9,000 Volunteers escorted it across the city through watching crowds to Glasnevin cemetery. It was a staggering show of strength by a group considered by many people to have been demoralized and disbanded after the rising the previous year.

A volley was fired over the grave and then Collins stepped forward to speak: 'Nothing additional remains to be said. The volley that we have just heard is the only speech that is proper to make above the grave of a dead Fenian'.

Collins continued his work for the National Aid Association, treating the beneficiaries with genuine respect, keeping meticulous accounts and bringing an energy to his tasks that few, if any, could try to emulate. But there was another, and nationally more important, part of his workload that only a select number of colleagues could see and help share. The task of reorganizing the Volunteers would be wasted without weapons to arm them properly. Despite raids for weapons, many units carried only hurleys or, at best, shotguns and outdated rifles. Collins made several trips to England to set up arms smuggling with IRB members in London, Manchester and Liverpool.

He had studied previous Irish risings and recognized to what extent espionage had been responsible for their failure. Throughout the centuries, spies had infiltrated every revolutionary organization, a relatively easy task in a small country like Ireland, where a careless word spoken at a fair or in a bar travelled

Kitty Kiernan, photographed in the back garden of The Greville Arms Hotel in Granard, Co. Longford. She would be part of a love triangle with Collins and his best friend, Harry Boland.

horse-drawn carts and in hackney cabs through the flag-waving crowds. De Valera had been chosen as the Sinn Féin candidate to fight an Irish Parliamentary Party member in a by-election in East Clare.

Again, Michael Collins mustered local support and de Valera won by a massive majority. This victory was followed by that of W. T. Cosgrave, elected in Kilkenny City. The people were clearly moving towards Sinn Féin and its ideals. De Valera was elected president of the party. The Volunteers had begun training again and there were increasing numbers of arms seizures by them in different parts of the country.

In August, 1917, the British authorities in Ireland unwittingly, or hamfistedly, presented Sinn Féin with a major propaganda triumph. Thomas Ashe, a schoolteacher and president of the IRB, together with two colleagues, were court-martialled under the Defence of the Realm Act for making speeches 'likely to cause disaffection' and sent to Mountjoy Prison.

Members of the first Dáil photographed in 1919 after Collins (2nd left front row) had freed Eamon de Valera from a gaol in England. For obvious reasons, Collins didn't want to be photographed. He was persuaded to sit for this picture for reasons of posterity.

FAR RIGHT
The shooting of the two policemen in Co. Tipperary by Dan Breen and his unit heralded the beginning of the IRA's military campaign.

quickly to the headquarters of the British spy network, Dublin Castle. The eyes and ears of this network, especially in villages and the countryside, were the members of the Royal Irish Constabulary, who reported all snippets of information to the Dublin Metropolitan Police's political section, 'G' Division, based at Great Brunswick Street (now Pearse Street) Police Station. Some 'G' Division detectives roamed freely around the city, following those suspected of disloyalty to the Crown, or meeting informants and taking notes. Other 'G' men were positioned at railway stations or docks to watch the arrivals and departures. At the end of each working shift, all the 'G' men would transfer their notes and reports into a large ledger-type book held at the police station so that all members of the division would have access to the same information. This served as a communal cross-

reference and also avoided unintentional encroachment on the work of a colleague, which might jeopardise months of intelligence gathering. All important reports were dispatched to Dublin Castle for sifting and correlation. The system was simple, crude even, but very effective.

In March, 1918, Collins was introduced to a member of 'G' Division, Ned Broy, who had offered his services as a spy. Broy was acting as a clerk in Great Brunswick Street Police Station, with daily access to the main report book. Broy was a nationalist who saw his 'G' man work as unpatriotic. Since 1916, he had volunteered information to other members of Sinn Féin but they, understandably, had treated him with suspicion and did not encourage his efforts. Michael Collins instinctively trusted Broy from the moment he met him. However, he also knew that he could have

These men worked
in Dublin Castle
itself, the nerve
centre of British
intelligence

dust cover over it, was the famous Michael Collins. He asked me if I was still willing to help. I said, "Yes", and he said, "Good. We want you to go back to Dublin Castle". "Oh God", I said, "I'd do anything but go back to that bloody place". Collins said, "Look, the British trust you and we trust you. If you really want to serve the Cause, go back". so back to the castle I went.

The most amazing recruitment to Collins' spy network was his own cousin, Nancy O'Brien. She had been working for the telegraph service of the Post Office in London and had been transferred to the rebuilt and refurbished GPO in Dublin. Late in 1918, she was summoned to the office of the deputy head of the telegraph service in Dublin, Sir James MacMahon.

According to Collins' nephew, also called Michael Collins, Nancy was told by MacMahon that certain messages from Whitehall in London had been seen by Michael Collins before the officers for whom they were intended had received them. Whitehall and the Post Office had studied her personnel file and believed that she had 'no connection with these upstarts who would tilt at the British Empire'. They wanted her to be be responsible for decoding messages between Whitehall and Dublin Castle.

After work that evening, Nancy spoke to Collins whose first reaction was: 'Christ, how did these people hang onto their empire for so long and achieve so much, when they would put a cousin of mine in a job like that!'

For the next two years, that cousin would spend many of her meal breaks in the lavatory of the GPO, copying the decoded messages and tucking

Broy shot if the 'G' man showed any indication of being a double agent.

Collins recruited two more 'G' men, Dave Neligan and Joe Kavanagh. These men worked in Dublin Castle itself, the nerve centre of British intelligence in Ireland. Neligan did not join the group until 1920, after he had resigned from the detective unit in Dublin Castle. Like Broy, he had offered his services to Sinn Féin but had been turned down. He hated his work in the Castle and, on the advice of family and friends, left the police force and returned to his native Kerry. Collins eventually heard about his original offer of help and asked him to come to Dublin to see him. They met in a room over a bar in Henry Street.

Neligan recalled that first meeting. 'I was brought upstairs by the bar owner to this room which smelled of stale beer, and there, sitting at a table with a dirty

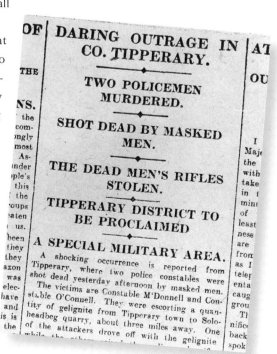

Superficially to many who met him, Collins was a hurly-burly character, given to explosive outbursts of temper

them into her underclothes to smuggle out to Michael Collins.

The 'G' men working for Collins were invaluable. They advised him on the 'mentality' of the intelligence establishment, how it operated and, especially, what it planned to prevent a recurrence of armed rebellion. Dublin Castle, like many in Sinn Féin and the Irish Volunteers, assumed there would be a standing battle similar to 1916. But Collins was planning something far more widespread and devastating.

He set up 'drops' in various parts of Dublin so that his newly-found spies could leave information at different locations to avoid detection as a result of following set routes and patterns that might be observed by those involved in counter-espionage at the Castle. These 'drops' included everything from shops to private homes, from railway stations to business offices.

The workload of Michael Collins was staggering. As well as his job with the National Aid organization, he cycled around the city each day delivering instructions to one group of Volunteers, receiving progress reports from others, and meeting emissaries from out-of-town units. By early evening, he would arrive at the regular rendezvous of senior Volunteer officers,

Vaughan's Hotel in Parnell Square, to begin a series of secret conferences and write dozens of letters, or travel out to houses in the suburbs to meet with political colleagues.

He enjoyed a beer or a whiskey but disliked drunkenness. The slip of a boastful tongue in previous generations had caused many downfalls. He was canny, too, in how much information he allowed any individual to have. He created a chain-link system of operation in which each person had sufficient knowledge to perform a specific task but not enough to connect that task with another individual, to carry him or her from one stage to the next but not, necessarily, to another person. If anyone was questioned, the overall network would not be endangered. Later, however, as the extent of the work increased, he was forced to divulge more to fellow senior officers.

His own memory was phenomenal. He remembered names, dates, times and quantities months after he had first received the information, much to the discomfort of colleagues who tried to bluff their way through an argument. This facility, which he developed for obvious security reasons, was even more annoying to British operatives who raided premises used by Collins and his organization in the hope of finding incriminating documents.

Superficially to many who met him, Collins was a hurly-burly character, given to explosive outbursts of temper with sufficient expletives to cower the most stubborn of men. But, just as quickly, the tantrum would dissolve into a broad grin or raucous laughter, and might be accompanied by a bear-like hug of reassurance.

One man who suffered these mood swings more than most was fellow Corkman Joe

Crowds gather outside Mountjoy Gaol to pray for hunger striker Thomas Ashe. After six days, he was forcibly fed and died as a consequence. His coffin was escorted to the cemetery by 9,000 Volunteers.

O'Reilly, who had met Collins in Frongoch and was later recruited by him to help with the National Aid Association. O'Reilly, who was a much more gentle man, was devoted to Collins and tolerated verbal and physical abuse that few other men would have countenanced. Despite this nerve-wracking lifestyle, O'Reilly would undertake any chore asked of him, no matter how dangerous or arduous

Like O'Reilly, many of Collins' men would also have to endure his moments of pressure-relief, when they would be subjected to 'grabbing a bit of ear', regardless of their mood. They would storm from the room afterwards, battered, bleeding, angry and humiliated, yet they would invariably return the following day to find Collins seemingly unaware that he had inflicted any pain whatsoever upon them. It was a measure of the man and his personality and the enormous loyalty he managed to engender, thay they returned at all.

Women, too, loved this brawny young man. Those

Collins, was soon doting on him as she might a son.

This remained Collins' home until 1922 and was often raided by the British. Miss McCarthy would give him a signal when it was safe to enter, and Collins would often wait in Dilly's home across the street for the all-clear sign. Dilly would play the piano for him while he waited and the friendship blossomed into romance. They enjoyed tram trips together to the seaside north and south of the city.

She was 17 when Collins, aged 25, moved into 'Aras na nGael'. She would later become aware of Kitty Kiernan's involvement with Collins, although she doubted whether Kitty ever knew of her relationship with him.

According to her daughter, Mrs Dorothy Heffernan, Dilly received hundreds of letters from Collins over the next six years. She kept the letters until her later years, when she destroyed all of them except for one note, which she gave to Mrs Heffernan as a souvenir. It was sent in 1917 and on the top right-hand corner was written '44. Saturday Morning'. In the note, Collins asked whether Dilly minded 'altering the time to 8.30 this evening'. It was signed, 'In Great Haste, With Love, etc., Michael Collins'.

Collins would often wait in Dilly's home . . . for the all-clear

British soldiers guarding a bank in the midlands of Ireland.

who knew him were infatuated by his good looks, infectious sense of humour and the gentleness and thoughtfulness he invariably showed despite the pressures of his work and schedules.

One such young woman was Madeline ('Dilly') Dicker, who caught the eye of Collins when he returned from his accounting job in London in 1916 and took up lodgings at 44 Mountjoy Street, Dublin. Called 'Aras na nGael', the house was run by a Miss Myra McCarthy who, like all women who met

Dilly saw Collins for the last time two days before he died. 'I'll be back, Dilly', he told her.

At the end of March, 1918, the last year of the Great War, the British army in France came under tremendous pressure when the Germans, under Erich von Ludendorff, shattered the line in the Arras sector and advanced 65 kilometres (40 miles), taking 80,000 prisoners. It seemed the British would be pushed back to the English Channel.

An Irishman, Field Marshal Sir Henry Wilson, Chief of the Imperial General Staff, urged the government to introduce conscription in Ireland. Already thousands of Irishmen were serving in regiments in the British army, but a call-up of all able-bodied men would provide many more.

Immediately after the Military Service Bill had been pushed through on 16 April, the Irish Parliamentary Party withdrew its members from the House of Commons in protest. It was an opportunity for Sinn Féin to unify nationalists. Dublin's lord mayor, Laurence O'Neill, called a meeting in the Mansion House which was attended by representatives of all aspects of Irish nationalism as well as the Labour Party. The assembly agreed upon an anti-conscription pledge, drawn up by Eamon de Valera,

which was to be signed by churchgoers the following Sunday and vowed, 'To resist conscription by the most effective means at our disposal'.

Catholic bishops, called upon to add their collective voice to the pledge, issued a statement which, although more tempered, managed to greatly influence public opinion. It claimed that conscription was an oppressive and inhuman law that the Irish people had a right to resist by every means that were 'consonant with the law of God'.

Part of that resistance came through the efforts of the Labour Party, who called for a one-day suspension of work throughout the country. Shops, businesses and theatres remained closed, trains did not run, and a protest rally was attended by all the leading nationalists who were told that conscription was 'declaring war on the Irish nation'. In Cork, 20,000 men pledged themselves to ignore any call-up. A local Franciscan, Father Matthew, declared publicly that conscription would be 'in direct violation of the rights of small nations to self-determination'.

The conscription issue had united in spirit, if temporarily, the two strands of nationalism – militant and moderate. Thousands of people now joined the Irish Volunteers to resist any forcible call-up. It was a dangerous stand-off for the British and they had to show determination. Lord Wimborne, Lord Lieutenant of Ireland, was replaced by the much tougher Field Marshal Lord French, and he was given the title of Lord Lieutenant-General and General Governor of Ireland.

But to avoid a backlash of public opinion in the United States, the first shots in Ireland

Conscription was 'declaring war on the Irish nation'.

FAR LEFT
Michael Collins and the famous bicycle.

LEFT
Notice for Ireland's 'most wanted man'. A sum of £10,000 was offered for Collins, dead or alive.

BELOW
Dan Breen, one of the toughest IRA leaders. When he died in 1969 his body still carried a bullet which hit him almost fifty years before.

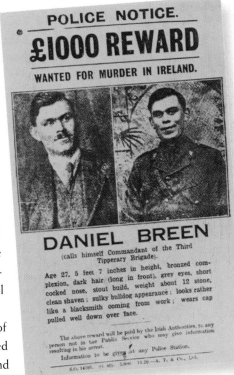

Vinnie Byrne at the age of 20 when he was a member of 'The Twelve Apostles'. Note the outline of the handgun in his jacket pocket.

would have to be seen to have been fired, or ordered, by Sinn Féin. Using powers granted by the Defence of the Realm Act of 1914, the first of a number of such emergency provisions, Lord French applied increasing pressure. Drilling and the carrying of arms by the Volunteers were, of course, banned immediately, but so, too, were Irish language classes, Irish dancing, athletics meetings and Irish football matches.

At this stage, Collins became a 'wanted' man. He had been arrested by 'G' men at his Dublin office after returning from Granard, County Longford. There he had made a speech 'likely to cause dissaffection'. He was taken to Brunswick Street Police Station and then to Longford, where he was charged. He jumped bail and from then on had a price of £10,000 on his head, dead or alive. Surprisingly, Dublin Castle had only poor photographs of Collins for identification purposes, and this, together with his ability to joke and chat with the military and police at checkpoints around the city, allowed him to stay at large.

An example of how he bluffed his way through these situations was remembered by a senior officer of a rural unit who had visited Collins in Dublin. That evening, making their way across the city on a jarvey car, they were stopped for questioning. The out-of-town man, aware that he was in the company of one of the most wanted men in the country, was terrified. Collins muttered from the side of his mouth: 'Act drunk!'. As they were being searched, Collins entertained the military with bawdy jokes and bad language, which soon had them all laughing. He and his 'drunken' companion were waved on their way.

Collins, now Adjutant-General of the Irish Volunteers, wore the ideal disguise for travelling on his bicycle around the busy capital: a smart, dark suit, highly polished shoes, a fine wool overcoat and trilby hat, and a briefcase full of papers relating to a 'front' business which would satisfy the closest scrutiny and questioning. His appearance and demeanor classified him as part of the commercial section of the 'establishment'. He never showed any annoyance and always had kindly exchanges with the men operating the checkpoints. After one such exchange of banter, a British soldier, patting Collins on the shoulder, said to him: 'Well, you're a decent sort, anyway!'

In May, the British were presented with a chance for a major round-up of Sinn Féin figures. The previous month, a German submarine had landed an Irishman, Joe Dowling, in Galway Bay in the hope of establishing a link with Sinn Féin. He was arrested shortly after he stepped ashore. The incident became known in British circles as the 'German Plot', a plan to

Some of the apostles. Left to right: Michael McDonnell, Tim Keogh, Vinnie Byrne, Paddy Daly and Jim Slattery.

attack Britain from the rear. A list of senior Sinn Féin members was drawn up by Dublin Castle, and raids throughout the city and suburbs were planned for the evening of 17 May.

Collins' spies in the Castle alerted him and he told as many colleagues as possible to stay away from their homes. However, most of the leading members were arrested that night, including Eamon de Valera and Count Plunkett. Sean McGarry, the general secretary of the Irish Volunteers, had already been arrested at his north Dublin home when Collins arrived on his bicycle to warn him about the raids. All told, 80 people were taken across the Irish Sea to gaols in England.

Still, in the climate of armed rebellion, London and Dublin hesitated about enforcing conscription in Ireland. The threat of call-up vanished on Armistice Day, 11 November, 1918. With peace now reigning in Europe, hundreds of Irish Volunteers drifted away from the organization. But the question of Home Rule was still unanswered, and it remained a serious threat to the stability of the United Kingdom. Prime Minister David Lloyd George proposed a degree of

Irish independence, from which six of Ireland's 32 counties would be excluded. These six northern counties were predominantly Protestant-populated. For Irish nationalists, especially the half a million Catholics who would find themselves on the other side of the border from their fellow Irishmen, this was a totally unacceptable arrangement.

Emphasizing the militant mood and what the general public considered to be a Sinn Féin victory over conscription, a general election in December of that year destroyed the moderate Home Rulers, the Irish Parliamentary Party. They retained only six of their original 80 seats. Sinn Féin won 73 out of 105 seats, giving them a majority in every county except four in the north of the country. Michael Collins reflected: 'Gone forever were policies which were a tacit admission that a foreign government could bestow freedom, or a measure of freedom, upon a nation that had never surrendered its national claim'.

Lloyd George proposed a degree of Irish independence, from which six . . . counties would be excluded

An artist's impression of a typical Flying Column, 'Men of the South – Flying Column' by Sean Keating, now exhibited in the Crawford Municipal Gallery, Cork.

The Irish people had to wait until the New Year to hear whether Sinn Féin's victorious candidates would attend or boycott the House of Commons in London. For 36 of them, there was no choice. They were in English gaols at the time of the election and were still imprisoned. On New Year's Day, 1919, mass meetings were organized throughout Ireland to demand the release of all internees, including the newly-elected Members of Parliament.

In the middle of January, Sinn Féin announced that instead of attending Parliament in London, an independent, republican Irish parliament would be established, called Dáil Éireann, with Eamon de Valera as its president. It was opened in Dublin's Mansion House on 21 January by Cathal Brugha, a squat, tough Dubliner who was an ardent supporter of armed rebellion. He was deputizing for Michael Collins who was in England formulating a plan to free Eamon de Valera from gaol. 'We are now done with England – let the world know it', Brugha told the cheering assembly.

Michael Collins was elected Minister for Finance and, more significantly for the Irish Volunteers, Director of Organization and Intelligence.

The structure of the Irish Volunteers was along British army lines of squads, platoons, companies, battalions and brigades. The strength of each company was usually between 70 and 100 men. There were four to seven companies in each battalion and three to six

battalions in a brigade.

Lord French estimated the strength of the Volunteers, or Irish Republican Army (IRA) as they had now become known, to be 100,000. According to Collins, its effective strength was never more than 3,000.

The quality of leadership varied, and some units, rather than obtaining armaments through raids on police stations, relied on Dublin to supply them with armaments (Raids on private homes had been prohibited by headquarters since March, 1918.) Some officers who called upon Collins to plead their cases wished they had never made the journey. After a blistering tirade, they would be sent scurrying back to their battalions, resolved to overcome their shortage problems in their own way, or in the way he 'suggested'. But Collins did recognize the fact that some units were unable, for reasons other than inertia or ineptitude, to equip themselves adequately, and so he set up secret munitions and bomb-making factories in order to meet demand.

Many units, such as the Third Tipperary Brigade, helped themselves. On the morning the Dáil first met, 21 January, 1919, Sean Treacy, Vice-Commandant, Dan Breen, Quartermaster, and seven other Volunteers killed two members of the Royal Irish Constabulary. The policemen were escorting a horse-drawn cart carrying 50 kilograms (112 pounds) of gelignite to a stone quarry at Soloheadbeg near Tipperary Town. According to Breen, the policemen were ordered to put up their hands, but, instead, grabbed their rifles and were shot dead by the raiding party.

These killings heralded the real beginning of the War of Independence, which would last three years.

Collins, meanwhile, had arrived in England to help Eamon de Valera to escape from Lincoln gaol. De Valera had asked another prisoner, Sean Milroy, to draw a postcard showing a drunken man with a giant key outside his hall door. The caption read: 'I can't get in'. The reverse side of the card depicted the same man in gaol a year later. He was peering through a keyhole and saying: 'I can't get out'. The drawings depicted the exact measurements of the actual master key and keyhole in the prison doors. De Valera had obtained a wax impression of the key for Milroy to copy. The card was sent out to the relative of another trusted prisoner. From the postcard template, a key was fashioned in Dublin and, in the style of comic book farce, sent inside a cake to de Valera in gaol.

On the night of 3 February, de Valera, Milroy and a third prisoner unlocked gate after gate with the key

He set up secret munitions and bomb-making factories

Commandant-General Tom Barry, leader of West Cork's famous Flying Column.

until they came to a small door in the outer wall. Collins and Harry Boland, having cut through a perimeter fence, were waiting on the other side of the door with a duplicate key which they inserted from the outside. It snapped in the lock. This was a moment of despair, but de Valera put his key into the lock from the inside and it pushed out the broken key and opened the door. Harry Boland wrapped his fur coat around de Valera and put his arm on his shoulder to escort the lanky escapee past other 'courting couples' in the area of the prison.

In June, de Valera sailed to the United States to seek recognition for the new republic and to float an American loan.

The first meeting of the Dáil, reaffirming Pearse's 1916 proclamation of a republic, brought London's attention back sharply to Ireland and shook the Dublin Castle authorities into frenzied activity. In the

next six months, more than 18,000 people were arrested, but Collins, having failed to appear in court in Longford to answer the disaffection charge, was still on the run and, thanks to tip-offs from his 'G' men spies about raids, moving freely around the city. He also had contacts through the Irish Republican Brotherhood around Ireland and overseas. In March, he had become president of this most secret and determined organization.

Liberty Hall in Dublin, the former headquarters of James Connolly's Citizen Army, being raided by Auxiliaries. On this occasion it was a 'nuisance' raid, taking band equipment away to demoralise its Republican owners.

FAR LEFT
The gathering of forces to combat Michael Collins. An R.I.C. Constable is flanked by two Auxiliaries, with a Tommy alongside.

The Cairo Gang, brought to Ireland by British Intelligence to track down Collins and his officers. The photograph, taken in Dublin Castle, was sent to Collins by one of his spies with numbers to identify the gang members.

He was audacious to the point of being foolhardy. He demanded that Ned Broy bring him into the 'G' Division headquarters itself, Great Brunswick Police Station, to see the confidential files for himself. Late one night, the two men slipped into the station and spent eight hours examining the information gathered on political and military activity around the country. After Collins and the very relieved Broy had left the building at seven o'clock the next morning, the 'G' man's heart almost stopped when Collins realized he had left some papers behind and insisted on returning to get them.

Information gleaned by Collins from Broy, Neligan and his other spies and contacts, convinced him that defensive tactics would not be sufficient in the future. The British intelligence system in Dublin Castle, a hash of military, police and secret service personnel whose diverse backgrounds had, in the past, led to incompetence through bickering and jealousies, were now forced to unite in the face of escalating guerilla activity, and because of pressure from their masters in London. Like it or not, they would have to accept some sword sharpening through an influx of seasoned intelligence men who had plied their trade in other sensitive areas of the empire.

The Royal Irish Constabulary, an armed force of 10,000 men and the Castle's 'eyes' in the countryside, were becoming isolated in their communities and suffering a spate of resignations. Recruitment had been reduced to a trickle. Informers, reliable barometers at times of previous unrest, brought tidings of an increasingly ugly mood in the towns and villages. The best solution the civil administration could muster was to make local councils financially responsible for any damage caused by the IRA in their areas. With widespread unemployment and low wages for those who could find any work, the stupidity of this proposal seemed unfathomable to the beleaguered authorities in the provinces.

Intelligence chiefs in London were more pragmatic: get Michael Collins, thus sever the head from the body of the IRA. Collins, of course, was aware of the proposed intensification and knew that he would have to move to meet it. He could not defeat the British in pitched battles but he could 'put out the eyes' of the intelligence service upon which the military relied.

The first moves were in the form of verbal warnings to a number of 'G' men whose activities were euphemistically described by one of Collins' men as 'too political'. More bluntly, they were instrumental in having key IRA or Sinn Féin personnel arrested. Some 'G' men heeded the warnings but others were too brave or stubborn. One of them was shot dead; another escaped, wounded, into his home but died later from his wounds.

Although he had embarked upon this ruthless path, Collins was also aware of a possible public backlash.

Although he had embarked upon this ruthless path, Collins was also aware of a possible public backlash. Republican newspapers and those sympathetic to the ideals of Sinn Féin were fed with appropriate propaganda. This, in turn, led to suppression and censorship by Dublin Castle. Such a kneejerk reaction, together with the obvious alarm caused by the killings of the 'G' men, confirmed to Collins that he was hurting the intelligence system, but he realized that

Smiles before the storms. Collins shares a joke with Harry Boland (left) and Eamon de Valera who would become his bitter enemies after years of comradeship.

London and Dublin would increase their efforts to smash his organization. The first killings had been carried out by volunteers, but he reasoned that a specialist unit was needed, a killing unit, who would react to orders efficiently and, most importantly, without qualms of conscience.

The squad came into being officially in September, 1919. Its members all belonged to the Dublin Brigade, which was commanded by one of Collins' closest allies, Dick McKee, a Dublin printer. McKee hand-picked eight young men whom he considered would be right for this dangerous and bloody work: Jim Slattery, Joe Leonard, Bill Stapleton, Pat McCrae, Paddy Daly, James Conroy, Sean Doyle and Ben Barrett. They were called to a meeting hall near one of Collins' haunts, Vaughan's Hotel in Parnell Square. McKee told them bluntly about the type of operations they would have to undertake. They would be assassins, commanded by a former Frongoch internee, Michael McDonnell, but operating under the direct orders of Michael Collins.

> **He reasoned that a specialist unit was needed, a killing unit**

All eight agreed to join the squad. A few months later they were joined by Tom Keogh, Mick O'Reilly and Vincent ('Vinnie') Byrne. Now a dozen strong, they soon earned themselves the nickname 'The Twelve Apostles'.

'We were soldiers, obeying orders, operating against professionals', Vinnie Byrne told the author. 'We believed we had to kill them. We were fighting for our country's freedom.'

The Twelve Apostles operated as an elite unit, separated mostly from the main body of the Dublin Brigade. Each man had, or was given, full-time employment in a trade or profession in which employer and work mates would provide an alibi during the raids and searches following an assassination. Unemployed men were easy and natural suspects at such times. Vinnie Byrne was a cabinet maker in a workshop near the city centre. This enabled him to take part in operations and slip back quickly to his work place before the inevitable round-ups began. The usual armament for an Apostle was a .45 revolver,

although Vinnie Byrne's preferred weapon was a Mauser pistol.

'We'd be told to plug a particular man, but how we did it was up to us. If we'd no information about his habits or movements, we'd watch him for a couple of days to see where he went and at what times. Usually, we'd have eight men on a job. One man would do the pluggin', with another man close by in case anything went wrong. The other six men would be spread around the area to give cover and to act as look-outs', said Byrne.

One such killing took place right outside Great Brunswick Street Police Station, the headquarters of 'G' Division.

Byrne told the author: 'This particular detective had been warned a few times about his political activity, but he wouldn't give it up, so I was sent to plug him. I knew that every morning he left the station at a certain time, so I waited on the far side of the street, a little way up from the station. When he came out, he crossed over to my side of the street. I walked towards him. My gun was still inside my coat, stuck into the waistband of my trousers.

'When we were about 6 metres (20 feet) apart we looked straight at each other. He knew somehow that I'd come to get him. Maybe it was the look in my eyes. He went for his gun in his side pocket but I got mine out first. Our lads never carried guns in their pockets because they always got stuck when you tried to get them out fast. This bloke was still trying to get his out when I plugged him in the belly. He sank down on one knee and finally got his gun out. He fired a couple of shots at me but he missed.'

And what did Byrne do? 'I

While bishops condemned the gunmen, many of their priests were nationalists and supported . . . the IRA

ran like hell, with yer man firing more shots after me,' he chuckled. The detective died in hospital later.

Summary executions were also carried out on informers. Some were shot without warning, others were taken to remote areas where they were allowed to kneel and say an act of contrition. As they prayed, they were shot in the back of the neck. Some were more fortunate. They were stripped, tarred and feathered and then tied to the railings of churches as a warning to others.

The Catholic Church in Ireland was split on the morality or otherwise of the killings. While bishops condemned the gunmen, many of their priests were nationalists and supported the objectives and activities of the IRA.

Vinnie Byrne told the author: 'I went to confession one day and told the priest I had shot dead a man. He asked me why and I told him, "Because he was a spy". The priest then asked me: "Did you believe you were right to do this?", and I said, "Yes, because I was a soldier and the man was one of the enemy". The priest smiled and said, "Good man yourself"'.

The ruins of Cork city centre, 1921.

The funeral of Terence McSwiney the 'martyred' Lord Mayor of Cork.

Michael Collins throws in the ball to start a hurling match in Croke Park, scene of the Bloody Sunday shootings by the Black and Tans.

Bloody Years

The Twelve Apostles, augmented by members of the Dublin

Brigade, gathered in the sunshine outside seven houses and

one hotel and waited for the clocks to strike. All of them

were armed with handguns. Some carried hatchets in case

they had to break down doors. At exactly nine o'clock, door

bells were rung and doors knocked. Once inside the

premises, the butchery began.

'A dangerous man.
. . . Care should
be taken that he
does not fire first'

Police bulletins described Michael Collins as 'a dangerous man' as the year 1920 began. They warned: 'Care should be taken that he does not fire first'. But, although he owned a revolver and an automatic pistol, Collins seldom carried either of them as he cycled around Dublin. Possession of a firearm was a capital offence and, besides, he could hardly hope to shoot his way out of a cordon of soldiers and policemen at checkpoints. Instead, he continued to submit himself good-humouredly to body searches, exchanging jokes with those who, literally, had Ireland's most wanted man in their hands.

Collins had set up a national loan scheme to fund the work of Dàil Èireann and its various ministries. With theatrical flair, he launched the loan on the steps of St Enda's School, which had been run by the Pearse brothers. The next-of-kin of the executed leaders of the 1916 Rising were the first to make donations. They queued to take receipts from Michael Collins, who signed the pieces of paper on the wooden block on which Robert Emmet, the leader of the 1803 Rebellion, had been publicly beheaded. Collins brought along a movie cameraman to photograph the launch at St Enda's, and the propaganda film was shown – sometimes at gunpoint – in cinemas and halls around the country.

The British tried to discover how the national loan funds were handled and deposited. Alan Bell, an elderly former resident magistrate, was brought out of retirement to conduct the investigation. Collins ordered The Twelve Apostles to kill him.

One morning in March, 1920, six members of the squad boarded the tram on which Bell was travelling from a suburb on the south of the city to Dublin Castle. One of the Apostles said to him: 'Your time has come, Mr Bell'. They took him from the tram and shot him dead in full view of the other passengers. No one tried to stop the killers, who walked calmly away.

The killings were not confined to one side only. In that same month, a group of men with blackened faces rushed up to the bedroom of the lord mayor of Cork, Tomas MacCurtain, and shot him with revolvers when he came to the door. Lord French circulated the story that MacCurtain, commandant of the Mid-Cork Brigade of the IRA, had been mudered by fellow republicans as a result of an internal feud. Few people believed the story.

An inquest jury, picked by the police, did not perform as expected. Instead of 'death by members of the IRA' or, at worst, 'by persons unknown', they returned a verdict of 'wilful murder against David Lloyd George, prime minister of England, Lord French, Lord Lieutenant of Ireland, Ian MacPherson, late chief secretary of Ireland, Acting Inspector-General Smith of the RIC, Divisional Inspector Clayton of the RIC, District Inspector Swanzy and some unknown members of the RIC'.

Locals were convinced that Swanzy was the officer who led the attack on Tomas MacCurtain. Collins had Swanzy tracked down to Lisburn, County Antrim, in the north of Ireland, in August of that year and shot dead. As a reprisal, Catholic homes and shops were burned down, and in a period of three days, 16 men and women died when rioting spread to other areas.

The spiralling violence was, however, at last bringing a response from the British government for the beleagured Royal Irish Constabulary and the authorities in Dublin Castle. From the end of 1919, advertisements began appearing in English newspapers for men willing to undertake – for a wage of ten shillings a day – a dangerous task in Ireland. Thus were gathered the first English recruits to the RIC. Many of them were ex-servicemen who had returned from the Great War to a jobless Britain and not, as Lloyd George had described it, 'a land fit for heroes'.

These men were not, as IRA propaganda claimed, riff-raff from English gaols. They were, simply, trained soldiers whose country could not afford to retain them, but who would be suited admirably to dealing with the IRA. Although these RIC recruits were not gaol-birds, their subsequent behaviour was worthy of the most hardened criminals. They would, they were told, make Ireland 'safe for the law-abiding'. However, operating with a free hand, no one was safe from their declared shoot-to-kill method, and they would earn abiding detestation.

When the first group arrived in Dublin from their depots in Liverpool and Glasgow, they wore a mixture of military khaki and dark police uniform. This likened them to the colouring of a well-known pack of hounds, the Black and Tans. The nickname stuck.

Although not publicly professed, their aim was to strike fear not only into the IRA but into the population as a whole. Their wrongful and convenient excuse was that a mass of Irish people supported the IRA and shielded them from the authorities. Indeed, the great strength of the IRA, and, indeed, later guerilla armies in other countries who would copy the model, was that they were anonymous, mounting attacks on police and military installations and then merging quickly among their fellow citizens. But most of those same citizens had no connection with the IRA, and would be too frightened to afford them protection. The Black and Tans were a crude weapon against such a rebel force and they acted crudely.

When the Black and Tans moved into an area where the local police station had been destroyed, they commandeered the house of their choice in the neighbourhood as a replacement. If an attack was made on the RIC or military personnel, they often conducted scorched-earth warfare on nearby towns and villages. Some people were burned alive in their homes; others, who escaped the flames, were bayoneted to death in the street.

Many years later, a Black and Tan described how, when on patrol in lorries in rural areas, they would overcome tedium by taking pot shots at farmers working in the fields.

An even more formidable corps was founded a few months later. They were recruited from among ex-officers of the British army and were called Police Auxiliary Cadets. Their former military ranks ranged from lieutenant to brigadier-general. They were paid a pound a day and wore khaki tunics, breeches and

Michael Collins standing in the ruins of his home in West Cork, burned down by the members of the Essex Regiment. 'They knew how to hurt me most,' he said. The destruction was ordered by Major Percival who, in the Second World War, surrendered the Singapore Garrison to the Japanese.

Arthur Griffith, on his first peace talks visit to London, with Eamon de Valera. The two men would differ on the terms of the Treaty and the Civil War ensued.

refusing to surrender in the face of far superior odds.

Officers and gentlemen they may have been in former years and in a different theatre of war, but in Ireland their probity was often lacking. Their frustrations were those of the Black and Tans, facing a shadowy enemy who ambushed and then disappeared. Trench warfare had not prepared them for these tactics.

Collins, of course, was not confining his activities to military warfare. Working primarily now at an office in Mespil Road, Ballsbridge, he had already overseen the organization of two underground newspapers, and would later set about opening a Sinn Féin bank to rival the British-approved establishments.

Cash and gold bars were frequently 'banked' in the home of Collins' friend, Batt O'Connor, in Brendan Road, Donnybrook, in the south of the city. A child's coffin was one of the preferred modes of transport for the shipping of gold. British soldiers and members of the Dublin Metropolitan Police were, understandably, loath to stop a hearse and open an infant's casket at a checkpoint. Many years later, an electrician working in the basement of the Bank of Ireland in College Green – about 200 meteres (220 yards) from Great Brunswick Street Police Station – discovered the coffin under a pile of broken furniture.

There were other, more outward signs of the demand for an independent Ireland. Throughout the land, Sinn Féin courts of law were established to administer their own justice in defiance of resident magistrates, and representatives were accredited to foreign countries, although these consuls were not officially recognized by the host government.

puttees and large tam-o'-shanter bonnets. They carried Lee Enfield rifles, with ammunition in bandoliers across their chests, and .38 Smith & Wesson revolvers in holsters on their waist belts. Many of the 'Auxies' had been decorated for gallantry in the Great War. They earned grudging respect from the IRA, who found them to be tenacious and brave in battle, often

Increasing numbers of municipal and other local authorities now answered to Dàil Èireann instead of Dublin Castle.

In the United States, Eamon de Valera, in the company of Harry Boland, had begun a campaign to float a £2 million bond loan. The money would be repaid when the Republic of Ireland had been officially recognized by the international community. But, in the course of his travels, he had fallen foul of some important Irish-American groups, and failed to get recognition from either the Republican or Democratic parties for the Irish Republic. However, despite these difficulties, he said he was ready to send about $3 million to Dublin, provided Collins could assure him that the money would be safeguarded.

Meanwhile, Ireland's most wanted man was travelling south almost weekly to Greystones in County Wicklow to deliver cash to de Valera's wife, Sinead, to feed her children.

Collins encouraged the military campaign in other parts of the country, although there were some criticisms that he, and other members of his GHQ staff, rarely visited units outside of Dublin. However, those who complained must also have been aware of the personal risk such trips, away from the relative anonymity of the heavily populated capital, would have carried. Instead, unit commanders or intelligence officers travelled to Dublin to give status reports or receive fresh briefings.

Late in 1920, those visits gave rise to the creation of the Igoe Gang, more commonly known as the Murder Gang. These 15 policemen, under the command of a West-of-Ireland head constable, had been drafted into the city from different parts of the countryside to identify known IRA officers for colleagues in Dublin Castle and 'G' Division. Most of them were Irish, but the group also included men originally from England, Wales and Scotland. All of them, including Igoe, used assumed names and their real identities were known only to a select few in the intelligence service at the Castle.

The Igoe Gang roamed the streets of Dublin . . . in the hope of finding the elusive Michael Collins

Their role as identifiers of IRA men was quickly expanded to that of killers. They were assured by Dublin Castle that they would never be brought to trial, even if eye-witness evidence was produced against them. Now both sides had units specializing in assassination.

Dressed in plain clothes, the Igoe Gang roamed the streets of Dublin looking for IRA men to arrest or assassinate, or to follow in the hope of finding the elusive Michael Collins. Arrested IRA men would be taken to Dublin Castle where they would be tortured in order to get vital information. Some IRA men did not survive the questioning. Others were executed after court martial.

The Gang met one IRA officer as he stepped from a train in Dublin and shot him dead on the platform. In a raid on a private house, the IRA man they had come to arrest was not at home, so they killed his father instead.

Collins, in turn, had members of the Igoe Gang 'fingered'. Members of the Apostles, together with other members of Dublin Brigade's active service units, would gather in two's and three's at designated points in busy streets. The lifting of a hat or the touch of a nose as the Igoe man walked by would be the signal of positive identification. The Apostles, mingling with shoppers, would move in, shoot the Igoe man, and then disappear into the horrified crowd. So the tit-for-tat killings continued, both sides convinced of the necessity and righteousness of their actions.

Black and Tans and the Auxiliaries patrolled the cities and towns in Crossley tenders – large, open-topped trucks. Their very presence managed to terrify the civilian population, not necessarily because of their trigger-happy methods but because of the knowledge that at any moment in time an IRA ambush could be launched, and everybody could be caught in the crossfire. IRA men waited on street corners and lobbed hand grenades into the vehicles as they passed by. To prevent this, the Crossley tenders were quickly fitted with wire-mesh coverings

the stillness of most nights was shattered by the sound of . . . screams and gunshots

Lady Hazel Lavery with whom Collins was alleged to be having a love affair. His defenders deny the story and say that without her political influence the Treaty talks would have been more difficult for both sides. (Detail from a painting by her husband Sir John Lavery).

so that hand grenades would bounce harmlessly off them. The IRA counteracted with grenades and bombs fitted with hooks to catch in the netting.

The aftermath of skirmishes was, inevitably, bayonet-point questioning and the searching of premises with attendant damage. A curfew was imposed, but the stillness of most nights was shattered by the sound of screeching tyres, shouted commands, splintering wood, screams and gunshots. Newspapers filled many column inches with reports of raids and shootings, and inquests into the mysterious deaths of men found when dawn had lit the streets and alleyways again.

Earlier that year, Michael Collins and his headquarters staff had greatly increased the effectiveness of the IRA outside the cities and towns. A brigade in the West of Ireland had demonstrated that a group of properly trained men could be summoned at short notice to ambush military and police convoys and then melt back into the community. Each brigade was, accordingly, ordered to set up such a unit – to be known as a flying column. However, the then practice of gathering IRA volunteers for once-weekly training sessions of a couple of hours' duration was totally inadequate to prepare men efficiently. So, the West Cork Brigade formulated a plan for five intensive training camps for battalion and company officers who, in turn, would train the men under their command.

The most famous of these officers was Tom Barry who would later rise to the rank of commandant-general. Barry had learned his soldiering with the British army in such far-flung theatres of war as Mesopotamia, Palestine and France. As a 16-year-old

Hazel Lavery's idealized drawing of Michael Collins.

recruit in 1915, he had known little about Redmond's promise of Home Rule if Irishmen fought for Britain or the appeal to save Belgium from the Germans. He had joined the British army simply to see what war was like. Demobbed in 1919, he returned to West Cork and soon became enthused with the aims of Sinn Féin. Later that year, he joined the local unit of the IRA.

The purpose of a flying column was to harass the military and police at every opportunity; to 'take the war to the enemy'. The word 'harass' encompassed killing or disarming the soldiers and the RIC, interrupting their communications and attacking their convoys and strongholds. As the operations of the flying columns increased, the identity of most individual members became known, and they could no longer live in their own homes. They became roving, full-time guerilla groups. Armed with an assortment of rifles and handguns, they carried leather or cloth ammunition bandoliers and were dressed in civilian raincoats and overcoats, with hats or wool caps.

Unlike their enemy, they did not have the benefit of a barracks or a billet and, exposed to the vagaries of the Irish weather, moved across country by night, often wading in rivers and streams to avoid detection. They lived off the land or sought food and shelter in 'safe' houses, that is, the homes of sympathizers. More often, they slept under hedges, but if a bed was offered, four or five men would share it, sleeping fully clothed except for boots. 'You got to know a lot about the other fellas,' an IRA man told the author.

They often spent days without food. When they could, they dug up potatoes or turnips and ate them raw because the smoke of a cooking fire would betray their position. According to the same IRA man, Poitín, the illicit whiskey, saved the lives of many flying column members. 'You could drink it,' he said, 'or rub it into your joints to keep out the cold.' Chuckling, he added: 'Most of us drank it.'

Tom Jones, Lloyd George's personal secretary, observed: 'The tenacity of the IRA is extraordinary. Where was Michael Collins during the Great War? He would have been worth a dozen brass hats.'

Above and right
The Treaty talks in
the Cabinet room of
10 Downing Street,
London. On one side
Collins and Griffith,
on the other Lloyd
George and
Churchill.

The attacks on RIC patrols and Black and Tan convoys and barracks continued, and the pursuit of intelligence-gatherers was ruthless. At times, no place or occasion was sacred. In the West Cork town of Bandon, an RIC sergeant was known to be Dublin Castle's principal source of information about local IRA activity. He knew he was a marked man and confined himself to barracks. He ventured out only once a week, to attend mass at the church just 100 metres (110 yards) from the barracks. An escort of Black and Tans brought him to the church gates each Sunday morning and then returned to their barracks once they had seen him safely onto holy ground. On 25 July, 1920, he thanked his escort and walked up to the church door. Two IRA men moved with him and shot him twice. The sergeant stumbled and fell, dead, into the porchway of the building.

Later that month, British soldiers captured Tom Hales, commanding officer of the West Cork Brigade, together with the brigade's quartermaster, Pat Harte. In Bandon barracks, members of the Essex Regiment used pliers and pincers on the men's lower bodies, and to crush their nails, in an attempt to get information.

After a couple of hours, Hales was unconscious and Harte had gone insane. The soldiers made them pose for a camera, waving a Union Jack. Hales was court-martialled and sentenced to penal servitude in London. Harte was sent to a local mental hospital where he died a few years later, still insane.

Apart from human loss, attrition was extended by both sides to the economy, both locally and nationally. Collins ordered the destruction of a hundred income tax offices, much to the delight of many people who had never shown much sympathy for his aims. The British retaliated by blowing up creameries and flour mills upon which farming communities depended for their livelihood.

When the IRA burned down RIC barracks, the Auxies and Black and Tans set fire to sections of cities and towns. They also targeted the homes of known IRA men or their supporters throughout the country. The IRA then burned the mansions and castles of the landed gentry, most of whom were pro-British or perceived to be.

Michael Collins' family homestead at Woodfield was destroyed by soldiers of the Essex Regiment in

1921. They arrived in the early hours of the morning of 1 April, under the command of Major Arthur Percival. The eight children in the house were being cared for by a young housekeeper while Collins' brother, Johnny, a widower, was in Cork attending a city council meeting. The eldest child was 12 and the youngest, Liam, was one year old. The children were allowed to take their bedclothes from the house but nothing else.

Liam told the author: 'The soldiers rounded-up the neighbours and, at bayonet point, forced them to throw straw into the house and pour petrol onto it, then set fire to it. In this way, the soldiers could say that Michael Collins' own neighbours burned down his old home.'

The wooden cradle in which Liam had been sleeping, made decades before by Collins' father, was retrieved temporarily but then thrown back into the flames by the soldiers. One of the girls, aged 11, had to be physically restrained from rushing back inside to save her schoolbag. The soldiers tried to set fire to the family's former home alongside, then used as a cow shed, but left before the flames had taken hold. This building still stands on the site, which has become a Michael Collins memorial centre. Black smoke marks on the interior walls are reminders of that night.

Collins, standing in the ruined building some weeks later, said: 'They knew how to hurt me most'.

The burning of houses and shops by the British was discontinued when pressure was put on Members of Parliament by Irish landlords. They were being burned out of their ancestral homes by the IRA. Throughout Ireland there are ruins today of once-beautiful castles and manors destroyed during that period.

Later, in 1942, Percival, by then a Lieutenant-General and nicknamed 'Rabbit' by his men because of his prominent teeth, unconditionally surrendered the Singapore garrison of some 90,000 men to a much smaller force of Japanese. Winston Churchill, who had told Percival to fight to the death, described the loss of the 'impregnable' fortress as 'a heavy and far-reaching defeat'.

However, for Collins in the early 1920s, the 33-year-old Percival remained elusive. Several attempts were made to kill him, but he was shrewd and lucky. A 'hit' unit followed him to England when he went on leave, but he stayed safely inside a military barracks for the duration of his visit. In Cork, an IRA man ordered to watch his movements was spotted. Percival and a group of men arrived and shot him dead.

Meanwhile, during 1920, a new and far more deadly foe had entered the arena. Colonel Ormond Winter gave himself the code-name, 'O', which,

Collins ordered the destruction of a hundred income tax offices

Bodyguard Emmet Dalton leads Michael Collins from their London headquarters during the Treaty talks.

although lacking somewhat in originality, was as good as any, as all code-names were made known immediately to Collins by his spies. Winter was sent by London to take over counter-insurgency operations. He was described, unkindly, by a senior British civil servant as a 'little white snake', although his appearance could have been created by the author of an espionage novel: sallow complexion beneath a receding and greased hairline, and small eyes, one of which peered through a monocle. A black cigarette holder completed the picture of this dapper man whom the IRA quickly called 'The Holy Terror'.

He took charge of yet another intelligence/assassination group, the 'Cairo Gang', who earned their nickname from their previous activities in Egypt and because they frequented the Cairo Restaurant near the centre of Dublin. Winter stayed in the Castle, filtering the information delivered to him and co-ordinating the activities of his 12-member group.

In addition, Winter set up a web of intelligence gatherers throughout Dublin. These were serving army officers recruited by the British secret service to work for him. They lived alone in flats or in small groups in suburban houses, mainly on the south side of the city. Their task was to pinpoint IRA officers and centres, glean information about them by bribing neighbours or domestic servants, and feed back this intelligence to Winter. He

The 'O' net was closing. It was just a matter of time

would decide what action would be taken against the targets, and when.

The Cairo Gang made some mistakes but this was inevitable. In the early hours of a September morning, the Gang arrived at the Exchange Hotel and shot dead a young man from County Limerick, John Lynch, in his bed. He may have been mistaken for the Cork senior officer, Liam Lynch, who would later become chief-of-staff of the IRA. The Castle said John Lynch had fired on police to resist arrest. In fact, he was not a Volunteer and did not have a gun, but he had just delivered a large sum of money for the Dáil loan, so there was a connection with Michael Collins. The Cairo Gang also arrested a number of Collins' senior intelligence officers but released them when they convinced their interrogators that they had no IRA connections.

But the arrests alarmed Collins. The 'O' net was closing. It was just a matter of time before it would close on Collins and his fellow leaders. One of those interrogated by Dublin Castle was Frank Thornton who had been held for ten days. The questions put to him convinced him that the Cairo Gang's knowledge about IRA activities and personnel was far wider and deeper than had, until then, been believed by Collins.

The killing of John Lynch garnered local newspaper coverage, but another death that year focused international attention on the situation in Ireland. Terence MacSwiney, sworn in as Lord Mayor of Cork in succession to Tomás MacCurtain, was arrested for possessing documents 'likely to cause disaffection'. He refused to recognize the court martial and went on hunger strike in Cork gaol. He was transferred to Brixton Prison in London, where he died after 74 days without food. Two colleagues who had been arrested with him died in Cork.

Londoners, who until now had, perhaps, shown little interest in republican aspirations across the Irish Sea, were moved by the self-sacrifice of MacSwiney.

Thousands lined the streets to pay their respects as his coffin, accompanied by a guard of honour of Volunteers, set out on its journey home. Lloyd George, at the behest of Sir Henry Wilson, Chief of the Imperial General Staff, diverted the coffin directly to Cork in order to avoid the international publicity that a stage-managed procession would have attracted in Dublin. But, despite this, the whole of Ireland came to a standstill, the Dáil having declared a day of national mourning.

The day after MacSwiney's funeral, Kevin Barry, an 18-year-old medical student, was hanged in Mountjoy gaol for his part in the ambush of a military lorry in Dublin. One soldier had been shot dead and two others died from their wounds.

Dublin Castle, through ignorance or indifference, chose 1 November as the day of execution. This was All Souls Day, when churches were packed for masses. Congregations throughout the country prayed for his soul. His youth, and the fact that the soldiers opened fire first, made Kevin Barry a martyr.

Soon after his death, a ballad about his capture and execution was being sung by both sides in the conflict. The author has a copy of the ballad, handwritten by a British soldier in the Curragh army camp, with the added warning, 'Not to be sung in public'. However, it soon became an anthem for freedom fighters everywhere and was sung by British and American soldiers during World War II.

Meanwhile, the Cairo Gang had been busy. In the previous month, they had tracked down Dan Breen and Sean Treacy, the men who had killed the RIC men in the Soloheadbeg raid for gelignite. Breen and Treacy were staying with a friend on the north side of

Dalton, ever watchful holds open the taxi door as Collins arrives in Downing Street. An aircraft was on constant standby in case the talks broke down and Collins had to make a quick escape.

Not going well. An angry Collins leaves Downing Street after a further round of talks.

Dublin when the Cairo Gang, supported by a large force of soldiers, surrounded the terraced house. Two intelligence men rushed upstairs to the top-floor bedroom and fired through the locked door. Breen and Treacy returned fire and killed both agents.

As Treacy made his escape through the window, Breen was hit in the spine by a bullet fired by soldiers advancing up the stairs to the room. He pulled the door open and stepped out onto the landing to meet the soldiers. One bullet grazed his forehead, two hit him in the calves of his legs, another lodged in his right lung and yet another passed through his thigh. He walked down the stairs, firing his handgun. The soldiers turned and ran before him, out into the street.

Breen returned to the bedroom, stepping over the dead intelligence men and a wounded soldier. He dropped from the window onto the roof of the conservatory and then into the garden. As he passed a greenhouse, he saw the bodies of two soldiers who had been shot by Treacy. A soldier appeared at a low wall and shot at Breen, but missed. Breen fired back and the soldier fell dead. Barefoot and with a broken toe, Breen

Collins being interviewed by a reporter on the steps of his headquarters in London.

made his way out onto the main road where he was confronted by an armoured car. He fired at the soldier in the open turret, who dropped down out of sight. Breen then made his escape through the grounds of a nearby college, and across a shallow river to a house where he was given first aid and taken to hospital.

The ambulance service later reported that they took away 13 bodies from around the raided house.

Sean Treacy escaped uninjured that night, but three days later was spotted and followed by a Cairo Gang member to The Republican Outfitters, a city centre drapery shop owned by Peadar Clancy, a senior IRA officer on Collins' staff.

The Cairo man sent for reinforcements which arrived just as Treacy was leaving the premises. An armoured car and two lorries filled with soldiers pulled up outside the shop. A Cairo man named Francis Christian, dressed in civilian clothing, jumped from one of the lorries and rushed towards Treacy who was about to mount a bicycle to escape.

'Here's the man we want', Christian shouted. Treacy drew his gun and grappled with a second Cairo man, Lieutenant Price, and shot him dead. Then he wounded Christian before a third member of the Cairo Gang came up from behind and killed him. The soldiers then fired their machine gun and rifles in the general direction of the dead Treacy, killing two civilians and seriously wounding a police constable.

Terence MacSwiney had said: 'It's not those who

can inflict the most but those who can endure the most who will conquer'.

At another time, Michael Collins' intelligence staff would have agreed with the sentiment but not now. If Collins and his senior officers were arrested or killed, the organization would be crippled. True, the IRA had field combatants, but without efficient counter-intelligence leadership it would be operating without 'eyes' and would be destroyed within weeks.

Collins acted quickly. He ordered a citywide intelligence operation to learn the names and addresses of those working for Colonel Winter's Cairo Gang. This was the first in a series of steps leading up to the event that became known as Bloody Sunday.

Frank Thornton, Dick McKee and Peadar Clancy were delegated to gather this information from spies and informants around the city. There were tell-tale signs of the involvement of particular British officers in covert activity. They did not belong, nor were they attached, to regiments based in Ireland at that time, they dressed in civilian clothes, and often left their houses after curfew and returned after dawn. Business connections, when investigated, were found to be either fronts or non-existent. Such men were immediately under suspicion, and their involvement with the secret service was substantiated by Collins' spies in Dublin Castle and in 'G' Division.

Sunday, 21 November, was agreed as a day of action because it was a day of rest, when officers were slow to rise, and because there would be a football match in Croke Park that afternoon with attendant crowds in the streets which would hamper searches and raids.

The night before, one of Collins' Dublin Castle spies, Dave Neligan, went to the Gaiety Theatre with Liam Tobin and Tom Cullen from IRA headquarters. Cullen produced the list of officers to be assassinated.

Neligan scanned the names and then said: 'Look next door'. Two of the officers who were to die were seated in the neighbouring box.

But later that night, there was an incident which, had it become known to Collins, might have caused the operation to be called off. Dick McKee and Peadar Clancy had been arrested in a raid by the

Auxiliaries and taken to Dublin Castle. Another young man, Conor Clune from County Clare, who had no involvement in IRA activities, had been taken from Vaughan's Hotel and he, too, was in custody.

As was confirmed later, the three men were tortured in order to divulge information about the IRA. The innocent Clune had nothing to tell. McKee and Clancy knew everything about the plan for the following day. Obviously, they were able to withstand the interrogation because, otherwise, the men assigned to be assassins would, instead, have been the victims of assassination themselves the next morning.

Had Collins known, would he have gone ahead, trusting McKee and Clancy not to have divulged

The Treaty concluded between Great Britain and Ireland, signed when Lloyd George threatened total war against the Irish.

Collins and Griffith
photographed
shortly after the
signing of the Treaty.
Both show the signs
of strain and
exhaustion and not
the elation that
better terms would
have produced.

information? Probably not, although those who knew him have argued about this ever since. A measure of the brutality of Dublin Castle interrogators can be gained from Collins' reaction to the news of the arrests the next morning. 'Oh God, we're finished now. It's all up,' he said.

The following morning, The Twelve Apostles, augmented by members of the Dublin Brigade, gathered in the sunshine outside seven houses and one hotel and waited for the clocks to strike. All of them were armed with handguns. Some carried hatchets in case they had to break down doors. At exactly nine o'clock, door bells were rung and doors knocked. Once inside the premises, the butchery began.

In one house, an officer pleaded with his executioners not to shoot him in front of his wife. She was pushed into another room and he was shot. In another house, the girlfriend of another officer threw herself protectively across him in the bed. She was pulled aside to give the gunmen a clear aim.

A kilometre away, an officer was dragged from his flat, screaming for help, and shot through the chest. A colleague who came downstairs to investigate was placed against the wall and the guns of the firing

RIGHT
Michael Collins on
the balcony of his
delegation
headquarters. He
said of the Treaty: 'I
have signed my
death warrant.'

squad were trained on him. The hand of one of them shook so much that he was a danger to everyone in the hallway. His gun was taken from him and the officer was shot by the leader of the group. The officer survived his wounds.

At the Gresham Hotel in Sackville Street (now O'Connell Street), another group of gunmen held up the head porter and demanded to know the numbers of the room occupied by Captain Wilde and Lieutenant McCormack. As the leading member of the group rounded a corner on the staircase, he was confronted by gunmen similarly dressed and armed. He fired immediately, shattering a floor-length mirror.

Wilde was shot in the doorway to his room, and McCormack died in bed, shot through the newspaper he had been reading.

In a house in Lower Baggot Street, another secret service man was shot as he tried to scramble out of his bedroom window. He had locked his door and was straddling the window sill when the assassins broke into the room. The pyjama-clad body lay hanging out the window until the ambulance service arrived.

In another house, a member of The Twelve Apostles, frustrated because his intended victim was not at home, angrily spanked the officer's mistress with a sword scabbard.

Vinnie Byrne was in charge of a hit unit assigned to 38 Upper Mount Street, the home of two officers, Colonel Peter Aimes and Major George Bennet. These men were the 'field' leaders of the Cairo Gang.

Almost 70 years later, Vinnie Byrne accompanied the author to that house (now offices) to describe what happened that morning in 1920. As we walked up the granite steps to the hall door, Byrne clutched the author by the elbow and said: 'I'd better watch meself here. I might be visited by the two lads'. Then he laughed.

'We went to mass in Westland Row and then strolled up here', he said. 'We waited outside on the pavement there until exactly nine o'clock and then rang the doorbell. A maid answered the door but she realized something was wrong and tried to shut it again. We pushed past her and demanded to know which rooms Aimes and Bennet were in.'

The maid indicated a ground-floor room. Byrne and his colleagues threw open the door. The officer in the bed immediately reached under his pillow for a revolver but quickly changed his mind when he saw the guns levelled at him.

He was bundled out of the bed and down to a room at the back of the stairs where his colleague was sleeping. Both men were made to stand on the bed, facing the wall.

Byrne went on: 'I said, "You two men have been sentenced to death and I've come here to carry out that sentence. May the Lord have mercy on your souls". Then we shot them and got out of the place as quickly as we could.'

An eyewitness described the bloody scene in one house as being 'like a badly conducted abbatoir'.

The bodies of 14 officers were removed by ambulances later that day, but these were official figures and the total number of dead may have been 20. Some of those who died were unconnected with the secret service and were shot either in panic or because they could have identified the gunmen later.

Dave Neligan recalled the 'panic, utter panic' in Dublin Castle when reports of the killings came in. 'They didn't know what was happening. They arrested thousands. It was the biggest blow they ever got.'

As the news spread, hundreds of military personnel and civil servants tried to seek sanctuary in the Castle, convinced they were all targets for Collins' gunmen. One secret service man, unable to stand the strain, shot himself.

Entire families arrived at the gates by any means of transport available, their personal belongings strapped to taxis, private vehicles and even jaunting cars.

One IRA man, Frank Teeling, was captured that morning but later escaped from prison. Another IRA man, who had no involvement in the shootings, was, nevertheless, tried for murder and hanged.

Collins said after the killings: 'For myself, my conscience is clear. There is no crime in detecting and destroying in wartime the spy and the informer. They have destroyed without trial. I have paid them back in their own coin'.

The secret service officers were later given a state

funeral in London, but behind his public utterances of shock and abhorrence, Prime Minister Lloyd George had secretly little sympathy for them. 'They got what they deserved,' he said, 'beaten by counter jumpers.'

But the killing was not over on that Sunday. In the afternoon, a company of Black and Tans arrived at Croke Park. They claimed afterwards that they were searching for the gunmen who had killed the secret service officers that morning. As they approached the ground, IRA look-outs opened fire on them. This has always been denied by those who were attending the football match.

Whatever the truth, the Black and Tans opened fire on the players and spectators with rifles and a machine gun. One player, Michael Hogan of Tipperary, and 11 spectators were killed. Fifty-seven other people at the match were wounded and 13 injured in the stampede for safety.

There would be three more deaths that day. McKee, Clancy and Clune were killed by their captors in the guardroom of Dublin Castle. An examination of their bodies later showed that they had been beaten, then bayoneted and shot. The authorities tried to explain the deaths by saying the three men had tried to escape by using hand grenades. How they got these grenades or had kept them hidden for more than 20 hours was never explained. In a clumsy attempt to support their claim, photographs were issued later by the Castle press office, showing 'the three men' sitting with bowed heads in the calm atmosphere of the guardroom and then springing for the steel-barred window, while their captors crouch behind overturned furniture.

> **Whatever the truth, the Black and Tans opened fire on the players and spectators with rifles and a machine gun**

To justify the death of the civilian, Conor Clune, the Castle described him as 'a lieutenant in the IRA'.

Dave Neligan reported to Collins that when the bodies were being loaded onto a lorry, one of the two officers responsible for their deaths went into a frenzied rage and battered their bodies and faces with his torch and revolver. Many years later, this man

wrote a novel, based on the events of that time, in which the hero receives a death threat for his 'murder of Clancy and McKee'. In real life, the author had actually received such a note.

Bloody Sunday had ended, but within eight days Tom Barry's flying column in Cork struck a devastating blow to the Auxiliaries, resulting in Lord French declaring martial law in three counties.

At half-past nine on the morning of 28 November, Barry set 36 men in positions overlooking the road at Kilmichael near the town of Macroom. Their task was to ambush two Crossley tenders carrying Auxiliaries ready for their daily raids on farms and villages.

When the tenders arrived at the scene just after four o'clock in the afternoon, they were attacked with rifles and hand grenades. The long-range fighting developed into hand-to-hand combat, with the Auxiliaries and IRA men clubbing each other with the butts of empty rifles and revolvers. At the end of the action, which lasted some 20 minutes, 18 Auxiliaries had been killed. Two IRA men had died and another had been fatally wounded.

The tenders were set alight and then Barry, seeing the shocked condition of his men, made them undertake five minutes of marching drill, up and down the road through the corpses to restore discipline. It must have been a macabre scene, with the flames from the

burning tenders illuminating the bodies of the dead and the white faces of the marching men.

Dublin Castle claimed the corpses of the Auxiliaries had been mutilated with axes, but this was never believed, especially by the colleagues of the dead men who had the opportunity to examine the corpses later.

The usual kind of reprisals followed the ambush. Farms and houses in the locality were burned, and the Black and Tans set fire to sections of Cork City. Two men, one a former British army officer, were thrown into a river and drowned.

The Auxiliaries then issued a proclamation which said that, because people who had appeared peaceful

The Dáil (Irish Parliament) meeting to discuss the Treaty. Its eventual acceptance led to the resignation of Eamon de Valera and the beginning of the Civil War.

housed the Local Government Board as well as the headquarters of the Inland Revenue. The idea, suggested by Eamon de Valera and approved by Michael Collins, was to throw both services into chaos. Without vital files, neither could function until their records were re-compiled.

Sections of the IRA held civil servants at gunpoint while others doused the files and furniture with petrol and set them on fire. But this took time, and the smoke and flames were spotted by patrolling Auxiliaries and soldiers before the raiders had the chance to get clear of the premises. One of those was Vinnie Byrne who, seeing the arrivals, threw his gun into the flames and slipped out of a side door to mingle with civilian onlookers. Others were not so fortunate. Six IRA men were shot dead by the Auxies.

Everyone at the scene, including Vinnie Byrne, was held at rifle-point and questioned. Those failing to satisfy the Auxiliaries were arrested and taken to Dublin Castle for interrogation.

Byrne told the author: 'I was wearing a cap, so I just put a pencil up behind my ear to give the impression of being a tradesman, which, of course, I was, officially. I was young-looking at the time and I told a British soldier who was holding a bayonet against my chest that I was an apprentice, sent to buy goods at the nearby suppliers.

'He searched my pockets and found a list of munitions written in a kind of shorthand. I had to quickly invent names, like 200 R's (rifles) were 200 Roundels and so on. Anyway, he must have been convinced because he just said, "Alright, get outa here".'

The Customs House fire was one in a series of incidents that led the British government, through

and loyal had produced pistols from their pockets, 'all male inhabitants of Macroom and all males passing through Macroom shall not appear in public with their hands in their pockets. Any male infringing this order is liable to be shot at sight'.

And so the violence continued into 1921. Between January and July of that year, 228 police and 96 soldiers were killed. In two months alone, 317 IRA members and civilians died.

Lloyd George was under great pressure, in Ireland and at home, to initiate a settlement. The pressure was increased further by the largest IRA operation – in terms of numbers – on 25 May. On that day, 120 Volunteers, including some of The Twelve Apostles, took over the Customs House in Dublin which

King George V, to open the door to a truce.

On a visit to Belfast on 22 June, the king said: 'I speak with a full heart when I pray that my coming to Ireland today may prove to be the first step towards ending strife among her people, whatever their race or creed. In that hope, I appeal to all Irishmen to pause, to stretch out a hand of forgiveness and conciliation, to forgive and forget, and to join in making for the land they love a new era of peace, contentment and goodwill.'

A month later, after a series of direct and indirect communications between Lloyd George and Eamon de Valera, a truce was agreed, coming into effect at 12 noon on 11 July. A month later, Eamon de Valera, Arthur Griffith and other delegates travelled to London. They were met at Euston Station by a jubilant crowd of well-wishers and supporters and escorted to Lloyd George's residence in Downing Street. Women knelt on the road outside, praying for a lasting peace.

Despite the promises the detailed talks offered, it was obvious when de Valera left London a few days later that he was not a happy man. He could not even manage a smile at those same crowds who had met him when he had first arrived. Although he returned to Dublin as a conquering hero, he knew that the partitioning of Ireland had already been agreed between Lloyd George and the Unionists in the north of Ireland, and that what was on offer to the remainder of the country was not even full dominion status.

The people waited and prayed. Eamon de Valera was re-elected president, and still they waited. At last, Lloyd George presented an acceptable formula for discussion: how the association of Ireland with the community of nations known as the British Empire may be best reconciled with Irish national aspirations.

Michael Collins, meantime, was fighting – and winning – another battle, for the love of Kitty Kiernan. As often as possible, he would travel to Granard in Longford. Despite these frequent meet-

The changing of the guard. British troops at a Dublin barracks are replaced by soldiers of the new Free State Army in 1922.

'The Big Fellow' armoured car, named after Michael Collins, enters Portobello Barracks (now Cathal Brugha Barracks) during the handover by the British Army.

ings, her other suitor, Harry Boland, was unaware that his great friend was also trying to win her heart. In the woods outside the town, Collins and Kitty would walk alone in the comparative safety of the British-IRA truce that had been agreed upon the previous month. After each meeting, and despite the great demands on his time, Collins sent Kitty an almost constant stream of letters.

'My Dear Kitty', he wrote, 'when I was speaking to you I had a kind of idea the Horse Show was coming off this week but, of course, it's next week and that's a very long time to wait to see you . . . . I'm really anxious to see you.'

But Collins was also aware that Kitty felt pangs of guilt about the unsuspecting Harry Boland. Collins

wrote to her: 'My Dear Kit, many thanks for your nice note. Harry is back here this morning. Will that entice you to come to town to give you that chance to which he's entitled? Yours, with love'.

Kitty was not easily won. She had a fiery spirit and strength of character irresistible to Michael Collins. Kitty visited him 'in town' (Dublin) several times, staying sometimes in a city-centre hotel but more often in the neighbouring county, Wicklow. At the Grand Hotel (now the La Touche Hotel) overlooking the sea at Greystones, the lovers found a haven from the pressures of political and military affairs, and from the glare of publicity that might have found them in Dublin. But how their relationship survived at all during those difficult times is hard to imagine. Indeed, as

the treaty negotiations approached, the strain could be seen in Collins' letters.

'My Very Own Dear Kit, am working almost asleep. You'll forgive scribble, therefore. Can't write any more. Am thinking of you and in a nice, nice way. Yours, I hope.'

It was assumed that Eamon de Valera, a skilful negotiator, would head the five-man delegation to London for the Treaty talks. But he argued that at a time of crisis, the head of state should remain at home. Arthur Griffith would lead the team which would include Michael Collins. This angered Collins, who argued that he was a soldier not a diplomat. But de Valera was insistent. Was Collins being set up for a no-win situation?

Tim Pat Coogan, author of *Michael Collins – A Biography*, the most detailed account of the man and his times ever published, told the author: '"Set up" is a rather pejorative term, but it is true that de Valera himself, in his career, kept his hand on everything. When he was negotiating subsequently with the British, he did it personally. When he was drafting the Irish constitution, he did it personally. He kept the tightest possible control on his cabinet and everybody around him. He must have known from his dealings with Lloyd George beforehand exactly what was there. And the fact that, for once, he did not want his hand on the talks, suggests that he must have known the gap was going to be uncomfortable, and he wanted to stay out of it'.

In London, most of the delegation, including secretaries and staff, stayed at 22 Hans Place. Collins, guarded by members of The Twelve Apostles, estab-

lished his headquarters at 15 Cadogan Gardens, West Kensington. With Collins was Emmet Dalton, who had fought with distinction for the British in the Great War. Since then, Dalton had been a member of Collins' military staff. He also was apprehensive about the London visit but for different reasons.

Dalton said: 'We, in the IRA, were annoyed about Collins going to London because it exposed him to the enemy. He had been sheltered up 'til then. It caused us a lot of worry, so it was decided by the general staff that we would purchase an aircraft that would be held at Croydon. The object was, obviously, to get Collins back to Dublin as fast as possible should the talks break down'.

Formal talks got under way at 10 Downing Street on 11 October, 1921. At eleven o'clock, Collins and his group entered the building. David Lloyd George's fellow negotiators wanted to avoid shaking Collins' hand, so the prime minister met the Irish delegation at the door of the Cabinet Room and ushered them directly to their chairs at the boat-shaped table. Arthur Griffith and Collins sat directly opposite him.

Negotiations would last two months and entail seven plenary sessions, 24 sub-conferences and nine meetings of special committees.

Each morning, Collins went to mass at Brompton Oratory and lit a candle for Kitty Kiernan. Often, he would return to Cadogan Gardens before his fellow delegates had wakened for the day ahead.

And he was keeping in touch with Kitty: 'Kit Dear . . . I did a journey of 8 kilometres (5 miles) to my sister's place for a letter from you. No letter. Honestly, I felt it terribly, but I do not believe that you failed to write, and won't believe it until I know. Goodbye for the day. Tough work before me. Every good wish and thought'.

Kitty wrote: 'My Very Dear Michael, I wonder how you are doing in London. Meet any nice girls that you liked? Did you kiss anybody since? I didn't. Didn't get the chance. You know I'm only joking. My

Collins . . . argued that he was a soldier not a diplomat . . . . Was Collins being set up for a no-win situation?

A huge meeting addressed by Collins after the signing of the Treaty. These rallies were frequently disrupted by the firing of shots by anti-treaty gunmen. The Treaty, argued Collins, did not give full freedom for Ireland but it was the first real step towards liberty.

INSET
Collins in full voice, arguing the reasons for the ratification of the Treaty.

love to you'. There were suggestions in their correspondence of sexual intimacy between Collins and Kitty, either real or imagined.

'I'd love to have you here', wrote Kitty, ' But we must be really good. No bedroom scenes, et cetera, et cetera, et cetera.'

There was speculation also, privately and publicly, about Collins' relationship with one of his most ardent admirers, Lady Hazel Lavery, the young wife of the renowned portrait artist, Sir John Lavery, who was 68 years old at that time. Lady Lavery, whose likeness would one day grace the Irish pound note, was one of London society's great beauties. That society chattered and speculated about a love affair between Hazel and Michael Collins.

Whether the two did have an affair is something that will never be known. Hazel's best friend was Anita Leslie, daughter of Sir Shane Leslie, a cousin of Winston Churchill. Collins would often visit the Lavery home, but Sir Shane Leslie had an explanation other than romance for those visits: 'We brought Winston and Collins together in Sir John Lavery's studio instead of a government building for private talks. They came to the studio on the pretext of having their portraits painted. It would have been quite impossible to get any kind of a treaty if it had not been for this arrangement between Winston, Lady Lavery and Collins'.

Lloyd George threatened the Irish delegation with 'immediate and terrible war' if they rejected the terms

Collins himself wrote to Kitty about reports of the alleged affair: 'You ought to have seen some of the papers here yesterday – "M. Collins in Downing Street with his sweetheart". The Laverys took me there in their car. Some of the correspondents recognized my friend, but the story was too good'.

Meanwhile in Ireland, Eamon de Valera toured the country, inspecting IRA brigades and encouraging recruitment in case the London talks broke down and brought a resumption of hostilities.

In London, Lloyd George and his team would not agree to an Irish republic. They would, however, offer dominion status. Most difficult of all for the Irish nationalists was the demand that they swear an oath of allegiance to the English king. De Valera sent a message to his team in London, stating that he would agree to external association with the Crown, but internal association involving declarations of allegiance, no.

Lloyd George threatened the Irish delegation with 'immediate and terrible war', if they rejected the terms on offer. Then, on 5 December, he gave them until ten o'clock that night to accept or reject the British terms. The deadline came and passed. At a quarter-past eleven, the Irish returned to Downing Street.

After further discussion, some details were finalized and then, just after two o'clock in the morning of 6 December, 1921, the two sides each put their signatures on the Anglo-Irish Treaty.

Later on that same morning, Lloyd George and his team went to Buckingham Palace to receive the congratulations of their jubilant king. But in another part of the city, Michael Collins was deeply troubled. Listening outside his room, his friends heard him pacing back and forth across the floor. At last, the footsteps were silenced. Collins had sat down at his desk to write to Kitty Kiernan.

'I don't know how things will go now', he wrote, 'but with God's help we have brought peace to this land of ours, a peace that will end this old strife of ours, forever.'

This guarded optimism was reserved for Kitty alone. To another friend he wrote what turned out to be a chilling prophesy.

'Think, what have I got for Ireland? Something she has wanted these past 700 years. Will anyone be satisfied at the bargain? Will anyone? I tell you this, I have signed my death warrant.'

War

and Death

'Nothing could bring home more forcefully the awful, unfortunate national situation at present than the fact that it has become necessary for Irishmen and former comrades to shoot such men as Michael Collins.'

Free State troops begin shelling rebel strongholds with field guns borrowed from the British. Several soldiers were injured when the guns recoiled because the inexperienced gunners had failed to bed-in the weapons on the street surface.

Collins is cheered as he arrives in a taxi for the formal takeover of Dublin Castle. Collins arrived seven and a half minutes late and was admonished by a senior British officer. Collins smiled and said: "After seven and a half centuries you're welcome to the seven and a half minutes."

The New Year of 1922 brought growing division in Ireland about the wisdom of signing the Treaty. At rallies throughout the country, those in favour of the agreement with Britain argued that it was the best deal possible: those against, including Eamon de Valera, claimed Collins and his fellow delegates had sold out to London.

Collins knew that he had advanced the military campaign as far as he could. There was a groundswell of public opinion demanding peace. Without the people, the 'people's army' could not be sustained.

In those early weeks, he and de Valera, arguing from different sides, spoke undeniable truths. Collins said of the Treaty: 'In my opinion, it gives us freedom. Not the ultimate freedom that all nations desire and develop to, but the freedom to achieve it'.

De Valera said: 'I am against this Treaty because it does not reconcile Irish national aspirations with association with the British government. I am against this Treaty not because I am a man of war but a man of peace. I am against this Treaty because it will not end the centuries of conflict between the two nations of Great Britain and Ireland. If the Treaty is ratified, the Volunteers of the future will have to resort to civil strife to complete the work of the past five years'.

Dáil Éireann, meeting in Earlsfort Terrace, began a series of long and fiery debates. After one particularly exhausting session, Collins wrote to Kitty Kiernan: 'This is the worst day I've had yet. Far, far the worst. May God help us all'.

But, gradually, more and more members of the Dáil put their support behind Collins and Griffith. At last, on 7 January, they approved the action of the Irish delegation in signing the Treaty with Lloyd

Collins leaves Dublin Castle after the formal exchange of administrations.

**FAR RIGHT
The worried expression of a man who knows there is 'unfinished business'. One battle has ended but there is now another fight to face.**

Show of force. Anti-Treaty Republicans move into Dublin to occupy key positions and herald the beginning of the Civil War.

George and his ministers. Just seven members carried the day in the end: the voting was 64 votes to 57. A provisional government was elected, with Collins as Chairman. De Valera resigned his presidency and Griffith replaced him.

Almost immediately after the Dáil had ratified the Treaty, British forces began to evacuate barracks and temporary billets around Ireland. The Black and Tans and the Auxiliaries were demobbed and shipped back to Britain, as pleased to be leaving as the Irish were to see them go.

Not so happy was General Sir Neville Macready, Commander-in-Chief of British Forces in Ireland. He looked with great unease at this hand-over of military installations and equipment, wondering whether the peace would hold and whether he would be called upon to reconquer the country. The formal hand-over of power and the final withdrawal of his army was not to take place until December of that year, so he planned a defensive arc that would straddle the River Liffey to the west of the city centre. The

> **'I'm delighted to see you, Mr Collins'. Collins chuckled and said: 'Like hell, y'are!'**

Royal Barracks (now called Collins Barracks) and his relatively small remaining force would form his front line.

For Michael Collins, the sign of real change was the evacuation on 15 January of Dublin Castle by the civil administration, partly crippled by the Customs House fire, and the departure of the remains of its intelligence network, which had been blinded by the assassinations on Bloody Sunday.

According to his nephew, also called Michael Collins, The Big Fellow arrived in a taxi for the Lord Lieutenant's handover ceremony seven-and-a-half minutes late. The British officer overseeing the formalities reproached Collins for his lack of punctuality. Emmet Dalton, standing nearby, expected an explosive riposte, but Collins just grinned at the officer and said: 'After seven-and-a-half centuries, you're welcome to the seven-and-a-half-minutes'.

The lord lieutenant was said to have extended his hand to Collins that day, saying: 'I'm delighted to see you, Mr Collins'. Collins chuckled and said: 'Like hell, y'are!'

The government of the new Irish Free State met in

An Anti-Treaty IRA man poses for the camera during the occupation of Dublin by 'Irregulars' in 1922.

the Shelbourne Hotel in April to draft a constitution. Eamon de Valera, meantime, toured the south of the country in the hope of gathering support for his anti-Treaty stance. The most republican elements of the IRA would have little to do with him or Sinn Féin. They had set up an independent army council to resume the struggle for a totally free and independent Irish state to include the six counties in the north which, under the Anglo-Irish Treaty, had remained part of the United Kingdom. In some parts of the country, the new Free State Army and the IRA almost jostled with each other to take over the barracks evacuated by the British.

During this time, Collins and Kitty became officially engaged to be married. The international press descended on the Greville Arms Hotel in Granard, County Longford, to interview Kitty and photograph her. The spurned Harry Boland wrote to her: 'Kitty, I want to congratulate you. Michael has told me of your engagement and I wish you long life and happiness'.

Simmering discontent with the Treaty boiled over on 14 April when a group of IRA men – or Irregulars as they were now called by their former colleagues – seized the seat of legal administration in Dublin, the Four Courts, and other buildings in the city centre.

Civil War life in Dublin. A priest escorts children to a city centre school, hoping the Red Cross flag will guarantee safe conduct.

Collins made no effort to remove them.

A general election on 16 June returned only 36 of de Valera's anti-Treaty candidates out of a total of 128. Six days later, Field Marshall Sir Henry Wilson was assassinated by two IRA men on the steps of his London home. The order had, undoubtedly, been issued by Collins during the previous year but forgotten by him when the truce came into effect.

Collins had won an election battle but now faced a war

The two men who carried out the killing of Wilson were said, wrongly, by the British, to be fellow travellers of those occupying the Four Courts. Lloyd George demanded that Collins remove the Irregulars from the Four Courts and other buildings in Dublin immediately. Winston Churchill told an angry House of Commons that if the occupation 'was not brought to a speedy end, we shall regard the Treaty as having been formally violated'.

Collins had won an election battle but now faced a war. He demanded the surrender of the men in the Four Courts but they refused. Emmet Dalton, Director of Operations, decided to shell the building. The British loaned him field guns which he placed at various points around the building and began a bombardment which lasted 48 hours. The British would not trust their former enemies with high explosive ammunition, so Dalton had to use shrapnel rounds

'which was like hitting the place with peaches'. A total of 375 shells were fired before the garrison finally surrendered.

Dalton then turned his attention to the other strongholds in the city. Irregulars had to be dislodged with machine guns, rifles and incendiary bombs. The battles raged for five days, reducing business offices and shops to the burning shells last seen during the Easter Rising of 1916.

Among the casualties of the Dublin fighting was Cathal Brugha, Collins' former close colleague but now bitter enemy. His outpost, the last to be overcome, was the Hamman Hotel in Sackville (now O'Connell) Street. He refused to surrender and

walked out into an alleyway at the back of the burning building, gun in hand, to advance on a Free State barricade. He was hit in the thigh by machine gun fire, his femoral artery severed, and he died that night in hospital. Eamon de Valera, fighting as a Volunteer and without rank, escaped capture and went into hiding.

The shots fired in Dublin were not the first in the Civil War but they did herald the outbreak of general fighting throughout the country.

A war council was set up by the Provisional Government. Michael Collins was appointed Commander-in-Chief with the rank of general. He resigned his cabinet position in order to devote him-

self to the war against his former comrades, the Irregulars (IRA). His headquarters were in Portobello Barracks, later to be renamed Cathal Brugha in honour of the man whom Collins had said was 'at worst a fanatic – though in what has been a noble cause'. As Collins received the daily casualty reports about men who had once shared that common cause, his sense of grief mounted. His niece, Una Mulhearn, told the author: 'He was completely heavy-hearted about the fact that brother was fighting against brother. Members of families shunned one another. It was a terrible tragedy'.

The Irregulars concentrated their efforts on cities and towns outside Dublin. The new army moved

**Above and left
The Four Courts
after constant
bombardment. The
British did not trust
the Irish Army with
high explosive shells
and, instead, issued
only shrapnel
rounds. 'It was like
hitting the building
with peaches,'
complained General
Emmet Dalton
afterwards.**

Eamon de Valera inspecting 'Irregulars' who believed the war against the British should have been continued.

the coast from Dublin to sail up the River Lee and capture Cork City, outflanking defences set mainly against attack by land. It was a repeat of operations carried out in other areas in previous weeks.

But on the following day, 12 August, President Griffith, exhausted and broken-hearted by the years of struggle, suffered a stroke and died. Collins helped carry the coffin of his old friend from the pro-cathedral in Dublin. Three hundred thousand people lined the funeral route to Glasnevin cemetery, mourning the death of a man who had spent a lifetime trying to free his country from foreign rule and, having achieved that, had only seen his fellow countrymen turn upon each other. Michael Collins would survive him by a matter of days.

On 19 August, Collins went to a church in Greystones, County Wicklow, to have his confession heard. Had he had a premonition?

against them, forcing them out into the countryside where they operated as flying columns or smaller guerilla units. In the south, however, Cork and its western neighbour, Kerry, stubbornly held out, the access roads and rail links mined or blocked. Dalton overcame the problem by sailing a huge force around

Michael Collins and Arthur Griffith at the wedding of General Sean MacEoin ('The Blacksmith of Ballinalee'.) Two years before, MacEoin had attacked Auxiliaries and Black and Tans who had burned several premises in Granard, County Longford, including the hotel owned by Kitty Kiernan, Collins' fiancée

Collins on an inspection tour of the Curragh Camp in 1922 with General Emmet Dalton (centre). After Collins' death, Dalton resigned his commission because he objected to the harsh treatment of Irregulars. He became a door-to-door encyclopaedia salesman and caused a stir when he called on the duty officer at the Curragh Camp to sell a set. The books are still part of the library in the Officers' Mess there. He eventually went into the movie business as a producer.

At six o'clock the following morning, he left Portobello Barracks in a small convoy. Officially, he was undertaking an inspection tour of the midlands and south, but, in reality, he was making a secret and desperate effort to stop the Civil War. He had, through mutual friends, already made contact with 'neutral' IRA officers, that is, men who had not taken either side in the war. Through these neutrals, Collins would attempt to discuss peace with the leaders of the Irregulars.

Some of those leaders had already been captured and were being held in Maryborough Gaol (now Portlaoise Prison). Collins spent an hour talking to them but, obviously unsuccessful, left in a vexed mood for County Limerick. He was suffering from a heavy cold and a kidney infection. He was in constant pain and discomfort and had to stop frequently on the journey. He was edgy, too. Watching his men removing a bridge obstruction near Kilmallock, a local man took the opportunity to take a souvenir snapshot of the famous Michael Collins. He approached quietly and the click of the camera made Collins reach instinctively for his revolver.

He was making a secret and desperate effort to stop the Civil War

After inspecting the Free State garrison in Newcastlewest, he travelled southeast to Mallow in County Cork and then, that evening, to the Imperial Hotel in Cork where Emmet Dalton had set up his headquarters after the capture of the city.

'I was concerned to see him there', Dalton recalled. 'I knew how boyish he was, and the warmth and extent of his heart. He had a devout love for the people in Cork. I told him he was taking an unnecessary risk being there, and he said, jocosely, "Surely, they won't shoot me in my own county?"'

The following day, Collins travelled some 50 kilometres (30 miles) with Dalton to Macroom, where he had some secret talks with an influential neutral IRA officer. That afternoon, he made the last entry in his personal diary: 'The people here want no compromise with the Irregulars . . . . Civil administration urgent everywhere in the south. The people are splendid'.

Back home in County Longford, Kitty Kiernan was extremely concerned about his health and safety and told him so. In the last letter he ever wrote to her, he explained: 'Kitty, you won't be cross with me for the way I go around, and if I were to do anything else it wouldn't be me and I really couldn't stand it. Somehow I feel that the way I go on is better. Please, please don't worry'.

One of those who met Collins in Cork City was

his nephew, Sean Collins-Powell, then a quartermaster sergeant in the Free State army. He and his mother met Collins outside the Imperial Hotel and went inside for tea. Two young soldiers were sitting side-by-side in the foyer, leaning up against each other, half asleep but supposedly on guard duty. Collins banged their heads together and walked on.

'He was a bit tired at that meeting', Collins-Powell told the author. 'Of course, he had a very severe cold, bordering on pleurisy, but he was in reasonably good form. He was a very serious fellow and didn't waste time talking about himself.'

At 6.15 on the morning of 22 August, Collins and Dalton set off from the Imperial Hotel. The convoy consisted of a motorcycle scout, a lorry carrying eight riflemen, two Lewis machine-gunners and two officers. Behind the lorry, Collins and Dalton sat in the back of a yellow, open-topped touring car, a Leyland Thomas, loaned to Collins by a well-wisher. The

Michael Collins carries the coffin of his old friend Arthur Griffith from the Pro-Cathedral in Dublin. Griffith, broken-hearted by the Civil War, died from a stroke in August, 1922.

The strain of bereavement. Collins at the funeral of Arthur Griffith. He, himself, had only 10 days to live

driving was shared by two soldiers. Bringing up the rear of the convoy was 'Slievenamon', a Rolls Royce Whippet armoured car. This carried another officer and four men, including the operator of a Vickers medium machine-gun in its turret. This escort was most inadequate for a commander-in-chief in territory teeming with Irregulars.

On this day, the convoy travelled again to Macroom to resume the talks with neutral officers begun by Collins the previous day. After that, the convoy travelled to Bandon via the tiny crossroads village of Béalnáblath (The Mouth of Flowers). Unknown to Collins, senior Irregular divisional and brigade officers had gathered in a farmhouse overlooking the village for a war council. The officer-in-charge was Brigade Commander Tom Hales (who had been captured, tortured and court-martialled by the British in 1920). When Hales was told about the Collins convoy, he immediately planned an ambush in case The Big Fellow should return from Bandon by that route. A beer bottle collection cart was commandeered and placed across the road, 750 metres (820 yards) on the Bandon side of Béalanbláth crossroads.

In front of this, a 30-millimetre-long (12-inch) mine, containing 3 kilograms (7 pounds) of explosive, was buried beneath the surface of the dirt road and connected to a detonating plunger on higher ground. Twenty-two riflemen were placed in position overlooking the road to await a possible return of the Free State convoy.

Also unknown to Collins, Eamon de Valera had stayed in a farmhouse close to the village the previous night, and had passed through the crossroads just half an hour after the convoy had first reached Béalnabláth. De Valera was also opposed to the Civil War, but the Irregulars' Commander-in-Chief, Liam Lynch, was reluctant to cease hostilities and, so, told his officers not to encourage de Valera in his efforts. Despite persistent rumour and gossip, there is no evidence to support the claim that de Valera was involved in the planning of the ambush then being laid for his former friend and comrade.

Collins, meanwhile, had reached Bandon, travelled on to Clonakilty for lunch, then to Roscarberry, and onwards to Sam's Cross for a meeting with his relatives. Collins told a local officer that he was 'going to put an end to this bloody war'. At Skibbereen, he had more talks and left there at five o'clock in the afternoon to return to Bandon for tea. At Bandon, Collins had a detailed briefing from the local Free State commander, Major-General Sean Hales. Thirteen

Collins pictured two days before he died. He was watching his men removing a bridge obstruction when the photograph was taken, the click of the amateur cameraman's shutter making him reach instinctively for his gun. The tension and strain of the journey can be seen in his face.

The last photograph taken of Collins before he died. He is huddled into his greatcoat in the rear of the open-topped touring car with Emmet Dalton (nearest camera) as they leave Bandon for Béalnabláth. Collins had only 20 more minutes to live.

kilometres (8 miles) away at Béalnabláth, Hales' brother, Tom, fighting on the other side, was waiting for Collins to reappear.

After tea at Lees Hotel (now The Munster Arms), Collins and his convoy set off for Cork via Béalnabláth. He had less than half-an-hour to live.

In Béalnabláth, Tom Hales had sent most of his ambush party back to Long's public house at the cross-roads, convinced by the lateness of the hour that Collins had taken another route to Cork City. With six or seven men, he began the task of removing the mine and barricade. A look-out was posted in a lane overlooking the main road in case any Free State patrols should appear.

The Collins convoy reached the area just after seven o'clock, 15 minutes before sunset. A drizzle had begun to fall, and a mist drifted across distant fields. Collins, still suffering from his severe cold, huddled into the collar of his greatcoat. The driver and co-driver noticed that he and Dalton had lifted their rifles from the floor and now held them between their knees as they reached the gently curving road into the Béalnabláth valley.

The look-out in the overlooking lane had heard the engines of the vehicles in the convoy but was unsure about their identity until the motorcycle scout, Lieutenant 'Jeersey' Smith, rounded the bend. The look-out fired some shots at the convoy, both as a warning to his colleagues at the barricade and to alarm the convoy.

Dalton yelled at the driver of the touring car:

The convoy enters Béalnabláth (The Mouth of Flowers) in West Cork on the evening of August 22nd, 1922. Lieutenant Smith leads the way and 'Slievenamon', the armoured car, brings up the rear. Michael Collins and Emmet Dalton are in the yellow touring car. (Scene from author's television documentary 'The Shadow of Béalnabláth'. Photo by Tom Holton, RTE Stills).

RIGHT
Michael Collins lying beside 'Slievenamon'. Commandant Sean O'Connell whispers an Act of Contrition into his ear (Scene from 'The Shadow of Béalnabláth'. Photo by Tom Holton, RTE Stills).

FAR RIGHT
The scene of the ambush, Béalnabláth, a few days later. The 'x' marks the spot where he was shot.

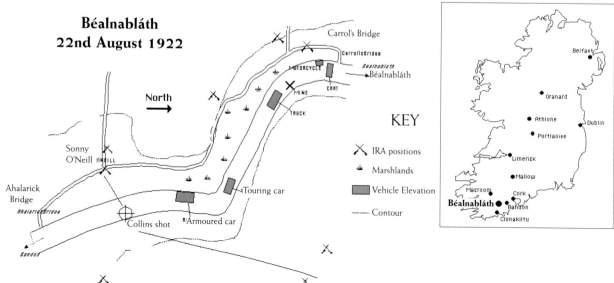

Béalnabláth
22nd August 1922

KEY

✕ IRA positions

🌿 Marshlands

▬ Vehicle Elevation

—— Contour

Michael Collins, is laid out in Shanakiel Hospital in Cork before transfer to Dublin.

Collins' death mask.

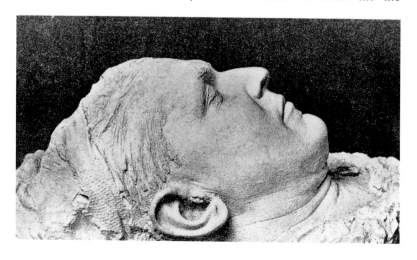

'Drive like hell!'. But Collins leaned forward and put his hand on the driver's shoulder. 'No, stop, and we'll fight them!', he countermanded.

All four men jumped from the car and took up firing positions behind the low bank bordering the road on the laneway side. Smith had, in the meantime, raced up the road on his motorcycle, followed by the lorry. At the barricade, the men fired at him as they retreated up into the lane. A bullet hit the handle-bars of the motorcycle, injuring Smith's hand. He turned the machine around and abandoned it in the ditch, then waved warnings to the lorry which had just arrived. The Lewis gunners opened fire on the retreating Irregulars while the remainder of the soldiers jumped from the lorry and divided into two sections. The first section ran to the barricade to move it aside while the second section gave them covering fire. The Irregulars ran along the overlooking lane in a series of sprints, firing at the men below, and then diving again for cover. They were under constant fire from the Lewis and rifles.

After a few minutes, the Free State men also moved up the lane, pushing the Irregulars towards Collins and Dalton at the other end of the skirmish area. At that spot, about 450 metres (490 yards) distant, the armoured car reversed a little to get into a better firing position with its Vickers machine gun. The Irregulars said later the bullets of the machine gun clipped the bushes above their heads as they lay flat in the lane between sprints.

Lieutenant Smith and Commandant Sean

O'Connell, the officer in charge of the convoy, made their way back along the road to inform Collins and Dalton that the road had been cleared should they wish to proceed.

On a sloping hillside to the right of the Free State men nearest the original barricade position, three separate and unconnected groups of Irregulars had joined the battle. The first was led by Mike Donoghue of Glenflesk, County Kerry, and was making its way home after losing Cork City. Unaware of the ambush plan, the group was drawn to the hillside by the sound of gunshots. Another two Irregulars also heard the shooting and made their way to the scene. The original ambush riflemen, who had been at Long's public house, returned to help their colleagues. At the Bandon end of the convoy, where Collins and Dalton had been firing side by side, another group of Irregulars, on its way home to County Waterford, was also drawn in. All this happened in the 17 minutes that had passed since the first shot fired by the look-out.

By now, Michael Collins was dead.

The armoured car's machine gun had jammed several times. An inexperienced officer had made a mess of loading an ammunition belt and this caused repeated stoppages. In one of these lulls, the pinned-down Irregulars took the chance to move further along the lane. Collins saw their movement and left Dalton and the protection of the roadside bank and moved around the bend to fire from the cover of the armoured car. When the Irregulars ran again, he moved from the armoured car to the centre of road. Standing upright, he fired a few more shots.

Up in the lane, Denis O'Neill, more commonly known as 'Sonny Neill', was covering his com-

Lying in State in City Hall, Dublin, with an honour guard of officers.

Collins' brother, Sean, grief-stricken, leans on the coffin in City Hall.

panions. He could not resist the foolhardy and reckless standing target. He aimed his Lee Enfield rifle and fired. The bullet entered the front of Collins' head on the hairline, passed through his brain and exited explosively behind his right ear. He fell face down on the road, still gripping his rifle.

Firing from the lane had now stopped. The Irregulars had escaped. Dalton, O'Connell and Smith rounded the bend to seek out Collins. They found The Big Fellow 'with a huge gaping wound at the base of the skull' and beyond human help. Dalton lifted Collins' head and tried to apply a field dressing to the ugly wound. O'Connell whispered an Act of Contrition into Collins' ear. The firing by the Irregulars, which had abated momentarily, now resumed. A bullet went cleanly through Smith's neck. There were no casualties on the Irregulars' side throughout the skirmish.

Collins' body was lifted into the touring car, his head resting on Dalton's shoulder, and resumed its journey to Cork City. Because of blown bridges and blocked roads, the sorrowful trip took several hours and the convoy did not reach Cork until the early hours of the morning. The body was laid out in a small, top-corner room of Shanakiel Hospital which

The coffin is borne through the streets on a gun carriage.

The cortege moves down O'Connell Street and onwards to Glasnevin Cemetery.

RIGHT
Letter from Richard
Mulcahy, Chief of
the General Staff and
successor to Collins,
instructing the men
of the armed forces
not to seek reprisals
after Collins' death.

FAR RIGHT
The Cork Examiner
of August 23 1922
says it all.

General Liam Lynch,
Chief-of-Staff of the
IRA who was
mortally wounded by
Free State Troops on
a mountainside in
County Tipperary in
April, 1923. The
following month, his
successor ordered a
general ceasefire.

had been taken over by Free State soldiers after the capture of the city. Dalton sent a telegram to Army headquarters in Dublin advising that 'commander-in-chief shot dead in ambush'.

Liam Lynch, Chief of Staff of the IRA, who would himself die in the Civil War, complimented his colleagues in the 1st Southern Division on the action at Béalnabláth, but added: 'Nothing could bring home more forcefully the awful, unfortunate national situation at present than the fact that it has become necessary for Irishmen and former comrades to shoot such men as M. Collins'.

When news of the death reached Kilmainham Gaol in Dublin, a thousand IRA prisoners spontaneously knelt and recited the rosary for the soul of Michael Collins.

The uniformed body of Michael Collins was brought to Dublin by ship. It was embalmed by Dr Oliver St John Gogarty. He confirmed afterwards that there were two wounds caused by the fatal bullet – entry and exit. The body was first laid out in the chapel of the old St Vincent's Hospital where Sir John Lavery captured the sombre scene on canvas. His wife, Hazel, spent some time standing beside the tricolour-draped body and then left, weeping.

Tens of thousands of men, women and children queued to pay their last respects to Michael Collins as he lay in state in the City Hall beside Dublin Castle. Among those who filed silently past the open coffin were many British soldiers, his former enemies, wearing black armbands on their uniforms.

Even more people lined the route to Glasnevin on Monday, 28 August, when the coffin, carried on a gun carriage pulled by four black horses and escorted by thousands of Free State soldiers, made its way slowly to Glasnevin cemetery. In one of her last letters to Collins, Kitty Kiernan had written: 'I was terrified that you would take all kinds of risks and how I wished to be near you so that I could put my arms tightly around your neck and that nothing could happen to you. I wouldn't be a bit afraid when I'd be beside you, and if you were killed I'd be dying with you and that would be great and far better than if I were left alone behind. I'd be very much alone if you were gone. Nothing could change that, and all last week and this I've realized it and that's what makes it so hard'.

Hundreds of wreaths were carried on military cars draped in black crepe which followed the gun carriage through the silent streets, but only one floral tribute was permitted on the flag-covered coffin – a single white peace lily.

It was from Kitty Kiernan.

HEROIC DEATH OF MICHAEL COLLINS

IRELAND'S WOE.

NATIONAL HERO DIES.

KILLED IN AMBUSH.

STORY OF GALLANT DEATH.

MILITARY FUNERAL IN CORK.

BY STEAMER TO DUBLIN.

GENL. MULCAHY'S MESSAGE TO TROOPS.

GOVERNMENT'S APPEAL TO PEOPLE.

An appalling catastrophe has befallen the Irish people.

The Nation was plunged into grief yesterday morning when the almost incredible fact became known that General Michael Collins was dead. Though generally disbelieved at first, the news was but too true.

Cork was at once plunged into mourning. All the business establishments ceased work for the day, and all the trams stopped running.

The grief-stricken populace learned the facts of the calamity in a special early edition of the "Echo."

General Collins was shot dead by ambushers at Baalnablath, a spot situated between Cork and Macroom. With members of the Headquarters Staff General Collins left Cork, in continuation of his visit to various military positions in the South.

The party were proceeding to Bandon by bye-roads, accompanied by a whippet armoured car, when they were attacked by a large party of Irregulars.

An hour's fierce fighting ensued. The Irregulars lost heavily, but just before the attack was beaten off General Collins was shot through the head, and in a short time died. A despatch rider in advance was the only other person wounded amongst the National forces.

In a feeble voice he asked for Major-General Dalton, and this officer and General Sean O'Connell went to the dying hero, says our reporter. They whispered a few prayers, reciting the Act of Contrition.

The Commander-in-Chief's last words when he lay dying on the roadside were "Forgive them."

The body was removed—under fire—to the armoured car, and brought to the Shanakiel hospital, Cork.

At noon yesterday, the dead hero was accorded a military funeral from the Hospital to Penrose Quay. The body was taken to Dublin on the steamer Classic. Crowds who thronged the streets openly displayed their grief at the loss of a gallant Corkman and an Irish National Hero.

General Mulcahy, Chief of Staff, in the course of a message to the men of the Army, says:—"Stand calmly by your Posts, bravely and undaunted to your work. Let no cruel ac' of reprisal blemish your bright Honour. To each of you falls his unfinished work. Ireland, the Army serves, strengthened by its sorrow."

A message from the Irish Government says that Michael Collins "has been slain, to our unutterable loss—but he cannot die. He will live in the rule of the people, which he gave his great best to assert, and which his colleagues undertake as a solemn charge to maintain."

At Cork Corporation and Cork Harbour Board touching speeches were delivered, and arrangements were made to be represented at the funeral in Dublin.

DETAILS OF THE AMBUSH.

The party of National troops consisted of about twenty, most of whom were officers of high rank. They included members of the headquarters staff, who accompanied the Commander-in-Chief to the South, and Col. Comdt. Sean O'Connell, the officer commanding the bodyguard; Major General Dalton, commanding the troops in Cork, and Lieut.-Comdt. Dolan.

A despatch rider on a motor bicycle preceded the party. Immediately after him was the large special Leyland touring car belonging to General Collins, and in it were travelling the Commander-in-Chief himself, Major-General Dalton, Lieut. Conroy, and other officers. A Whippet armoured car and an ordinary open tender brought up the rear.

The ambush occurred near Beal-na-blath at 6.30 p.m. last evening, the fight lasting about an hour. Beal-na-blath is situated between Bandon and Macroom, about eight miles from the latter town, a few miles from Crookstown, and south of the main road on the south side of the River Lee from Cork to Macroom. The district is wild, rugged, and is situated amongst the hills. The roads in the vicinity are poor, being chiefly bye-roads, as Beal-na-blath is altogether away from the main roads.

It was the interruption of communication on the main roads which led the party to proceed to Cork from Bandon by this roundabout route.

The party of officers, which included several of Ireland's principal military leaders as well as the Commander-in-Chief, left the Cork headquarters of the army at 6 a.m. on Tuesday morning, and travelled nearly all the port of South Cork occupied by the National troops, and took in Skibbereen, Rosscarbery, and Clonakilty in the course of the tour. At each place the officer commanding the troops was interviewed, and the Commander-in-Chief viewed, and the officers wore the two piece's of a very hearty, enthusiastic yet spontaneous greeting, and shook hands from the officers, but from the troops themselves. Little did they know that they would never again see the man whom they loved so deeply and admired so much.

Bandon was the last position of importance visited and the party then decided to return to Cork. It was then late in the afternoon, and the officers, and men were worn out after their round day's work, which had soon commenced as early as six o'clock in the morning.

The Commander-in-Chief himself also has been very tired. From Sunday evening, when he arrived in the city, he had been hard at work day and night. On Monday night at midnight and before he retired, the men refreshed a few hours later to continue his exacting work.

Owing to the destruction of bridges by the Irregulars, and other main obstructions, the direct route from Bandon to Cork was not available. The party accordingly set out...

(continued)

...greatness as nothing else could have done. He said "Forgive them"—and then died.

The body was removed—under fire—to the armoured car. The Irregulars were by this time in full retreat, having sustained very heavy casualties and leaving many dead and wounded on the field.

The National party were obliged to leave the Leyland touring car, and it was in the armoured car that the remains were brought to Cork, being conveyed to Shanakiel Hospital. The sad procession reached the city between midnight and one o'clock yesterday.

When the body of the dead Commander-in-Chief was moved into the armoured car it was seen that Major General Dalton's uniform was saturated with blood, and it was at first feared that this officer had been wounded. Such however was not the case. The stains were the blood of the great leader, who had died in General Dalton's arms. With the exception of the calamitous loss of General Collins, and the wounding of the despatch rider, the National party suffered no other casualties.

REMOVAL OF REMAINS.

MILITARY FUNERAL.

A SAD PROCESSION.

Eagerly crowds wended their way to Shanakiel Hospital, where the body was lying, and long before noon the hill was packed with people, while all roads leading to the hospital were lined with people. On every lip there were expressions of horror at the tragic ending of a great and promising career, and in every heart the deepest sorrow.

Some persons were allowed to the hospital grounds and a few had the honour to enter the room where the body was lying in state to bid the last office of their cherished leader. Officers of the Army formed a guard of honour and the room was laden with floral tributes and choice blooms. His comrades in arms, including Major General Dalton, were present. Many citizens passed in, and having said a silent, heartfelt prayer, left, ill concealing their emotion. A number of clergy were also present, including Most Rev. Dr. Cohalan, Bishop of Cork; Rev. Dr. Scannell, Farranferris; Very Rev. Fr. Mackian, O.P., Prior, St. Mary's; Rev. R. Walsh, O.F.M.; Rev. Fr. Breen, O.P.; Rev. Fr. Glendon, O.P.; Rev. Fr. O'Regan, C.M.; Rev. W. O'Sullivan, C.M.

Meanwhile the troops were lined up along the sweeping avenue to the hospital. About noon, the prayers for the dead having been said by Dr. Scannell and the assembled clergy, the bit was placed on the coffin and removed to the hearse. The pall bearers were:—Major General Dalton, Col. Commandant Kingston, General Liam Tobin, Col. Commandant Byrne, Col. Commandant Sean O'Connell and Lt. Commandant Dolan.

The order being given to the troops to reverse arms broke the silence which settled down with greater intensity, and a sad scene that was deeply impressive passed as the coffin was brought out followed by a number of nurses carrying handsome wreaths. The hearse moved down the ranks of the troops, and the military funeral was on its way. It proceeded on to Sunday's Well, over Thomas Davis Bridge, Western road, Washington street, Patrick street, and down to Penrose Quay, where the remains were put on board to be taken to Dublin. There were repeated evidences of tribute to the memory of Michael Collins, and a sincere showing of the general sorrow aroused by his illustrious death.

The following representing Cumann na mBan: Miss B. Conway, Mrs. Herbe, Mrs. Coughlan, Miss M. Scannell, Miss J. Allen, and Miss M. Comerford.

SCENES ON QUAYSIDE.

When it became known in the city that the body was being taken to Dublin by the ss Classic, people in large numbers thronged the quays, and by the time the funeral cortege approached Patrick's quay and Merchants' quay were crowded. The approaches to Penrose quay were, however, guarded by National troops, and to prevent congestion, the public were not allowed nearer the Classic than the Brian Boru bridge.

The Classic arrived from Fishguard at 10.30, and the news of the death of General Collins caused intense grief amongst the passengers, many of whom were visibly affected. Intimation was immediately conveyed to the Steam Packet Company and Captain Harrison that the vessel would be required to convey the remains of the Army Chief to Dublin, and the necessary preparations were at once made.

At one o'clock an armed guard with a machine gun went on board, and a little later the armoured car "Slievenamon" with her crew arrived, the armoured car being also placed on board the vessel.

As the crowds became more dense, members of the newly-formed Cork Civic Patrol, under Mr Jeremiah Murphy, assisted the military in keeping the quays clear. Their task was, however, an easy one for the mourning citizens had only to be told that their presence on Penrose quay would hamper the troops and the general public who followed the coffin to get them to comply with the requirements of the patrols.

Shortly after one o'clock the funeral cortege passed slowly down Penrose quay. His Lordship Most Rev. Dr. Cohalan and several priests walked in front of the coffin, which was covered with the tricolour, and borne on a hearse drawn by a pair of black horses. Behind it walked the relatives and friends of the deceased, well-known public men and political sympathisers, and finally the troops with arms reversed.

And then occurred the terrible calamity which has plunged the whole nation into grief and mourning. The battle was nearly over. The Irregulars were on the point of being defeated in spite of their overwhelming numbers, their better position, and their great advantage. The firing had become more keen intense.

Suddenly the Commander-in-Chief collapsed and fell prone, struck in the head by a bullet. From the very first it was obvious that the wound was one that though mortally wounded, still drew a tear from the ground, encouraging his men to be magnificent bravery.

In a feeble voice he asked for Major-General Dalton, and this officer and General Sean O'Connell went to the dying hero. Kneeling beside him they whispered a few prayers, reciting the Act of Contrition, before General...

COMMANDER-IN-CHIEF'S CAR.

General Michael Collins' car, the Leyland light cylinder in which he was...

GENERAL MICHAEL COLLINS.
Commander-in-Chief of the Irish National Army.

Hogan, Dublin.

NEWS IN CORK.

GENERAL GRIEF.

The news of the appalling tragedy quickly spread throughout Cork and created a profound sensation. At first people would say that the report of General Collins' death might only be one of the many rumours, a number of a sensational character, that have been in circulation for some time past, but such hopes were quickly shattered, and it was then realised that a great Irish leader had lost his life in the service of his country. Grief was everywhere awakened by the death, under such tragic circumstance, of the most widely known and respected soldier in the South of Ireland's most illustrious sons.

During the day large crowds gathered in the streets, especially in the vicinity of the Imperial Hotel and Victoria Hotel, and horror as well as general mourning, was everywhere evident.

It was only the previous evening, that business had proceeded on the tour of General Collins was held by the people. General Collins certainly acknowledged this cordial reception which was removed as he proceeded on a journey that was to bring him to his tragic termination.

Throughout Cork all places of business were closed as a mark of respect to the memory of the Irish patriot. The tri-colour was flown at half mast from all the buildings occupied by the National troops, and general mourning was manifested throughout the city, and indeed, the whole of Ireland.

NEWS IN LIMERICK.

SORROW AND HORROR.

Our Limerick Correspondent wired last night—In Limerick the news of the death of General Collins created a profound sensation and a very deep feeling of universal regret. The first intimation of the General's death was when it was given around for at the early morning Masses in the churches. As the morning advanced the sad news became general; the feeling it created was visible in every face. In Limerick, as elsewhere throughout the country, the dead soldier-patriot was revered by the people, and this was only too evident during his recent visit to the city when everywhere he appeared in the streets.

The people feel that to the extraordinary death of General Collins they have suffered not only a national, but personal bereavement, and while he died to provide their honour at his death. Behind the outward calm of the city, there is a strong and deep sense of poignant sorrow that finds itself should be deprived in every one of its greatest leaders and statesmen—men at a time when she most needed his wise counsel and cheery optimism.

On learning of the tragic news, the Deputy Mayor (Councillor Paul O'Brien) wired to Alderman Cosgrave, Acting Chairman Irish Government—"The bravest and best is gone for ever. We want sincere sympathy to you. The word 'sincere' fails to describe my feelings."

Mr M. R. Laffan, Chairman, and Mr J. J. Quaid, Secretary, Limerick County Council, wired to the Irish Government—"Profoundly shocked at calamitous disaster to Ireland in death of General Michael Collins, and we offer to Government and relatives, on behalf of Limerick County Council, our sincere..."

MESSAGE FROM MR. CHURCHILL.

"Cruel And Wanton Act."

London, Wednesday Night—Mr Churchill to-night sent the following telegram to Alderman Cosgrave and the Provisional Government "I have to express to you, as acting head of the Provisional Government, the sorrow which I feel at the news of this cruel and wanton act which has deprived Ireland for the hour of trust of the leader she had chosen, and in whose hands, in my ordinary person, largely-heartedness, and cheery willingness to give that little help when most needed, not enduring friendships.

DUBLIN AGHAST.

SORROW - LADEN POPULACE.

THE LYING-IN-STATE.

(Passed by Military Censor.)

(From our Reporter.)

Dublin, Wednesday.

The appalling news of the death of General Collins, which only reached Dublin in the early hours of the morning, has created a profound sensation, and has sent a thrill of horror through the nation. Additional poignancy lent to his tragic passing by the fact that after the many remarkable escapes crowded into the last six years of his life, he was ultimately shot dead by a bullet of an Irishman, only a comparatively short distance from his native home outside Clonakilty.

When the news was circulated throughout Dublin by early morning stop press editions, a feeling of consternation was created, and the people read, stunned at the dreadful import of this sensational tragedy in the short space of ten days.

His last public appearance in Dublin was this day week, when he walked alongside General Richard Mulcahy in the funeral cortege of President Griffith. Though evidently feeling to the full the sorrowful emotion inseparable from that melancholy occasion, he looked in perfect health, and walked with firm tread and soldierly bearing, his face pale and stern, his head bent, his hands gripping fast the large leather motor gloves he was carrying.

During the week-end General Collins had two escapes from death, one being a deadly attack on his motor car near Stillorgan. On Dublin, when, fortunately, he was not in the car, and the other being a collision between his car and another at Dunlaoghaire, when he escaped unhurt. He left early in the week for the Southern area of hostilities, and nothing further was heard of him till this morning, when the people of Dublin, who loved and respected the soldier chief so much, were thrown aghast at the tragic tidings of his death.

The terrible news spread like wildfire, and by the time the people began to come down to town on the morning trams it was the sole absorbing topic of conversation. It was impossible not to notice the downcast pre-occupied sorrow-laden department of everyone, but details were of the most meagre kind, and people seemed to feel the poignancy of the tragedy all the more keenly as there was little about it beyond the terrible fact that the head of the Government and the army, the leading figure in the public life of the country, the man who was the war had been invited into eternity by the hands of ambushers.

The first confirmation of the news as General Collins' death was contained in the order issued to the turn of the army by General Mulcahy, Chief of the General Staff (of which the text appears elsewhere).

The remains, which are being removed to Dublin by sea, are expected to reach North Wall about 2 a.m., and it is understood they will not be brought ashore till Thursday, a guard of honour being placed in charge during the night. They will lie in state for a few days, and probably on Saturday the late Commander-in-Chief will be accorded a national funeral, with of course full military honours.

Messages of sympathy are already pouring in, amongst the earliest being from Mr Reid George, General Neville Macready his Lordship Archbishop Rev. Dr. Dublin, Archbishop of Brisbane, the Belgian and American Consuls, the Mayor of Wexford, his Lordship Most Rev. Dr. Clery, Bishop of Auckland, etc.

MR. COSGRAVE'S MESSAGE.

THE NATION'S RESOLVE.

(From our Reporter.)

Dublin, Wednesday.—Announcing a message of condolence on the death of General Collins from the International News Service, Mr Liam T. Cosgrave, acting Chairman of the Irish Government, says—"His death is a terrible blow to the Irish nation at a time when it stood in need of his every moral courageous guidance. Much as all must feel that the example of his life, impressed on the people's minds by this tragedy, will raise their spirit to face difficulties as he faced them.

"His death has sealed his seal, and before the tragedy of his death the Irish nation is resolved to bring this week of triumph."

Rialtas Sealadac na h-Éireann
(IRISH PROVISIONAL GOVERNMENT),
Baile Áthacliath.

GOVERNMENT'S MESSAGE TO PEOPLE.

UNUTTERABLE GRIEF AND LOSS.

Dublin, Wednesday.

The following has been issued through the Government Publicity Department:—

"People of Ireland: The greatest and bravest of our countrymen has been snatched from us at the moment when victory smiled through clouds upon the uprising of the Nation to which he had dedicated all the powers of his magnificent manhood.

"The genius and courage of Michael Collins lent force and an inspiration to the Race, brought the long fight against the external enemy to a triumphant end, which had become almost a dream, and swept before it the domestic revolt which tried to pluck from your hands the fruits of that triumph—your unchallenged authority in the land.

"In every phase of the awakened activity of the Nation—constructive, administrative, executive, military,—the personality of Michael Collins was vivid and impelling. He has been slain, to our unutterable grief and loss—but he cannot die. He will live in the rule of the people, which he gave his great best to assert and confirm, and which his colleagues undertake as a solemn charge to maintain."

TO THE MEN OF THE ARMY.

Stand calmly by your Posts, bravely and undaunted to your work. Let no cruel act of reprisal blemish your bright Honour. Every dark hour that Michael Collins met since 1916 seemed but to steel that bright strength of his and temper his gay bravery. To each of you falls his unfinished work. No darkness in the hour, no loss of comrades will daunt you at it.

Ireland, the Army serves, strengthened by its sorrow.

R. UA MAULCHATA.
Chief of the General Staff.

SKETCH OF HIS CAREER.

HIS LIFE FOR IRELAND.

Ireland is plunged into irreparable grief by the death in action of General Michael Collins, Commander-in-Chief of the Irish National Army. Only on Saturday week last was the country shocked and saddened by the demise of the President of Dáil Eireann, Mr Arthur Griffith. To us, only just over a week Ireland has to bear the loss of two of her greatest sons, and in silence their strong arms, great gifts of intellect and able statesmanship in the building of the Irish nation. Just as well of Michael Collins in Ireland that she not only collovned him, but put a price on his head. The reward for his capture was £10,000—the biggest ever offered. But money could not purchase the betrayal of the hero of the people, and the country, so more than could England trace his whereabouts, though true to his courage and daring, Michael Collins walked their midst, and travelled the country by motor and train through their midst.

There are many incidents related of this thrilling escapes as served at casinos, and of never the daring and courage that animated the man as well as his coolness and clear vision, contrast the most exciting contingencies. There were episodes that if put on paper and published in book form by Mr Collins would have made fascinating reading and supplied many comrades for the most chat truth in all times stranger than fiction. The secret of his success from very few such episodes related by his friends must be attributed to his cool nerves and intrepidity. On one occasion that agents of the British Government put their heads in him in Sligo to Dublin, and executed "a few hours" his work as in the London General Post Office...

BIBLIOGRAPHY

Barry, Tom, *Guerilla Days in Ireland*, Anvil Books, 1981.

Breen, Dan, *My Fight for Irish Freedom*, Anvil Books, 1981.

Bennett, Richard, *The Black and Tans*, Severn House, 1976.

Collins, Michael, *The Path to Freedom*, Mercier Press, 1995.

Connolly, Colm, *The Shadow of Béalnabláth*, RTE Television Documentary, 1989.

Coogan, Tim Pat, *Michael Collins – A Biography*, Hutchinson, 1990.

Dwyer, T. Ryle, *De Valera – The Man and the Myths*, Poolbeg, 1992.

Farrell, Brian, (Ed.), *The Creation of the Dail*, Blackwater Press, 1994.

Feehan, John. M, *The Shooting of Michael Collins*, Royal Carberry Books, 1987.

Gray, Tony, *Ireland this Century*, Little, Brown & Co, 1994.

Keogh, Dermot, *Twentieth Century Ireland*, Gill & Macmillan, 1994.

McHugh, Roger, *Dublin 1916*, Arlington Books, 1976.

Meenan, F.O.C, *St Vincent's Hospital*, Gill & Macmillan, 1995.

Neeson, Eoin, *The Civil War*, Poolbeg, 1989.

O'Donoghue, Florence, *No Other Law*, Anvil Books, 1954.

O'Rahilly, Aodogan, *Winding the Clock*, The Lilliput Press.

Ryan, Meda, *The Day Michael Collins was Shot*, Poolbeg, 1989.

Twohig, Patrick J, *The Dark Secret of Béalnabláth*, Tower Books, 1991.

Various authors, *The Irish Republican Digest*, Nat. Pubs. Committee, 1965.

PICTURE CREDITS

Michael Collins Association, London (with thanks to Michael Griffin): 2–3, 6, 6–7, 20–21, 28, 36, 53, 56, 94 right

Corbis-Bettmann: 64, 85

Cork Examiner: 48

Crawford Municipal Art Gallery, Cork: 40–41

Dáil Éireann: 4

Hulton (with thanks to Mick Farrelly): front and back endpapers, 9, 14, 16 inset, 20 above left, 21 inset, 22 below, 23, 24 inset, 24–25, 26, 26–27, 29, 30–31, 31 below, 32, 35 right, 37 left, 42, 44, 45, 49, 50 inset, 50–51, 54, 59, 60, 61, 62 above and below, 65, 70–71, 72–73, 73 inset, 74 inset, 74–75, 76 above and below, 77, 78, 79 above, 80 left, 80–81, 82 above, 82–83, 83 above, 84 above and below, 90 below, 91 above and below, 92–93, 93 right, 95

Illustrated London News: 58, 63, 68

National Library of Ireland, Dublin: 12 left, 12–13, 14–15, 16, 17, 18 left and right, 18–19, 22 above, 37 right, 43 above, 66–67, 69, 94 left

Private Collections: 10, 10–11, 33, 38, 39, 41 right, 87 below, 90 above

Pyms Gallery, London: 57

RTE (Cashman Collection): 34–35, 43 below, 46–47, 79 below

Map on page 88 drawn by M. J. Foote

Owen Hickey, Co. Cork: 87 above

Text copyright © Colm Connolly

First published in Great Britain in 1996 by
George Weidenfeld & Nicolson
The Orion Publishing Group
Orion House
5 Upper St Martin's Lane
London WC2H 9EA

A catalogue record for this book is available from the British Library.

ISBN: 0 297 93608 0

Designed by Paul Cooper
Picture Research by Tom Graves

Title Page

Medallion of Michael Collins by Sean Keating from the memorial at Sam's Cross, Clonakilty, Co. Cork.

Contents Page

A portrait of Michael Collins by Leo Whelan now hanging in Dáil Éireann.

To Hans and Iris Bieraugel.

For special assistance and information, the author thanks Michael Collins, nephew; Liam Collins, nephew; Michael V. O'Mahony; National Museum Of Ireland.